AuthorHouse™
1663 Liberty Drive
Bloomington, IN 47403
www.authorhouse.com
Phone: 1 (800) 839-8640

Published by AuthorHouse 05/31/2018

ISBN: 978-1-5462-3646-7 (sc)
978-1-5462-3647-4 (e)

Library of Congress Control Number: 2018904061

Print information available on the last page.

Front Cover Drawing by Daryl Rantis Lead Architect for Green Hammer

This book is printed on acid-free paper.

SUSTAINABLE HOMES

FOR THE 21ST CENTURY

MICHAEL ROYCE AND **RICHARD BENNER**

Table of Contents and Synopses of Chapters

CHAPTER 1: The Dream Touches Down

Two couples dream of living their values by building homes with three themes: co-housing, aging in place, and sustainability. They find a site and additional partners, but the Great Recession dooms their first effort. Sweeping the ashes aside, they apply lessons learned and discover an ideal site, which is eminently walkable and with good solar access. They choose a design-build firm to bridge the gap between design and construction, believing the choice will save time and money. The firm shares their values and specializes in passive house construction. They opt to self-finance construction to keep costs down.

CHAPTER 2: Shooting for Net Zero

The couples choose a site ideal for solar electricity. The combination of passive house design and solar electricity will achieve "net zero," they hope, generating more electricity than they need. They imagine privations: small windows and Jimmy Carter cardigans. Instead, passive house offers choices and tradeoffs, many of which produce real quality-of-life gains. They devote hours to finding efficient appliances to close the energy demand-supply gap.

Chapter 3: Aging in Place

The couples design their project with aging in mind because they want to stay in their new homes as they grow old. Starting with a walkable location near a grocery store, movie theater and other services and with good transit, they choose a co-housing model to ensure they will have friends next door to help them age gracefully. They include a common room where they can gather, exercise and dance and pay attention to detail: ground access to each unit from the street, master bedrooms and baths on the ground floor, walk-in showers, room for wheelchairs and levers for door handles.

CHAPTER 4: Living with Friends

The couples want to live with friends, but how closely? The design process helps them a find balance between social engagement and privacy. A common room and terrace will gather partners. Sharing furniture, chores, services and subscriptions will also draw them together. A courtyard with paths connecting units, the mailboxes and the recycling barn will generate casual encounters during the day. Individual patios screened by low vegetation and second-floor decks with railings will give them time apart. In informal gatherings with prospective partners, they discover similar values. To extend their good luck they add a "right of first refusal" to their bylaws, providing some control over second-round partners.

Developers' fees can be 10 per cent of project cost. The couples believe they can save money being their own, "citizen developers." They could tell prospective partners "no developer's profit." They give Green Hammer a budget of $2.25 million and begin the search for a construction loan. Partners in the project intend to pay off their shares of the loan when they sell their existing homes or convert their share to a mortgage. The recession renders their analysis academic: no bank is willing to lend for condos due to the recession glut. The couples settle on self-finance of construction using home equity lines of credit. Worried about attracting friends to the project, they work to cut costs during schematic design.

Development spawns a blizzard of documents: establishing a limited-liability corporation; the LLC operating agreement; contracts with Green Hammer; "Declarations" and Bylaws for the condo association. Several partners, who had practiced law for at least part of their working lives, are confident of their drafting skills, relying on models available at co-housing and condo websites. The non-lawyer partners remind them to send their drafts to a real estate lawyer. They negotiate a fair allocation of risk between owners and their design-build firm. Anxiety over their "citizen developer" status dissipates when the owner of Green Hammer decides to buy into the LLC to jumpstart construction. Partners add confidence by hiring a part-time "owners representative."

Green Hammer presents a site plan and floor plans and the partners launch into detailed design, expecting the design-build model will insert budget controls forcefully. Unit customization, code requirements and a recovering economy increase costs and require choices to keep to budget. Their thousands of choices – from stovetops to tile grout – complicate cost tracking. "Value engineering" (cost-cutting) eliminates the hot tub, the pergola over the terrace and the entry portal. The design-build model fumbles on occasion, and tensions arise between partners and Green Hammer. Contract negotiations bog down, but construction gets underway on a "limited notice to proceed." Partners learn how to make decisions.

Partners break ground with Dr. Wolfgang Feist, Director of Passivhaus Institute, late September, 2013. Surprises pop up: pilings are needed to support foundations in unconsolidated soils; undetected underground oil tanks appear; a survey reveals a neighbor's wall over property lines. More "value engineering" and schedule delays are unhappy necessities but the buildings pop up before their eyes. Heavy insulation wraps foundations and packs walls and ceilings, triple-pane windows and doors seal the buildings. These are passive houses! Photovoltaic panels clip onto the metal roof. Cabinets, flooring and kitchen islands appear. Partners are anxious to occupy.

CHAPTER 1: The Dream Touches Down

Two couples dreamed of designing and living in homes representing their values and looking to the future. Over a decade, this dream progressed from a hazy vision to a plan and eventually six homes built to emphasize community, environmental sustainability, and graceful aging.

The four of us, Richard Benner and Lavinia Gordon and Michael and Francie Royce, brought years of experience and a commitment to livable communities, bicycling, and public transit to the project. Michael was a plaintiff's attorney and ran a family renewable energy business and Francie worked for two Portland city bureaus, planning and transportation. Dick was a land use attorney working at a land use advocacy group and as director of the state land use agency. Lavinia worked as a lawyer for the region's largest private utility and managed the alternative transportation division for the city's transportation bureau.

We realized later, however, the most valuable experience we brought to the task was the time we had spent founding and serving on the boards or staffs of a dozen or more nonprofit environmental or service organizations. We knew how to do budgets and had suffered through countless strategic planning exercises with large groups of people while actually enjoying the process.

We wanted a walkable, bikeable neighborhood well-served by transit and retail, and homes which felt sustainable. This led us to Portland's close-in eastside neighborhoods whose commercial cores had once been linked by streetcars. These areas were recovering from the post- war rush to the suburbs. The notion of adding "roof tops" and maybe some storefronts was very appealing. We also started thinking about "aging in place" and sought a location and living environment in which we could age gracefully.

Concept to "Program"

The design process started with what we knew best: a strategic plan. Each of us distilled her or his vision to a one-page set of concept elements. Then we condensed our efforts into a single set of elements and principles:

> **Initial Concept**
>
> At least two, but no more than four stories.
>
> Possible retail, office or live-work space.
>
> At least six, but no more than 12 condos.
>
> Buildings to be green, sustainable and energy-efficient.
>
> Everything essential for aging-in-place on the first floor.

By spring 2005, we had a concept for a co-housing, aging-in-place, "green" condo project at a flat, walkable site well-served by transit and bikeways on the east side, with retail services (especially a grocery store) within a quarter-mile.

Ground-floor retail remained the most challenging concept element. Michelle Reeves, a broker active in the cool districts of eastside Portland, warned of difficulty for those with no commercial experience. Many parts of these areas had enough shops. The best thing we could do was to add rooftops - customers - to one of the recovering neighborhoods. We abandoned the retail element of our concept.

We roamed the eastside looking for property. The best sites had been purchased by developers several years earlier. The few remaining vacant locations were beyond our budget. We knew several developers who had done admirable in-fill projects around town, but they were soured on condos. The cost for construction defect liability insurance had risen dramatically in response to an outbreak of litigation. "Penciling" condos had become very difficult.

These dead-ends brought us new partners.[1] Friends Jim Piper and Roberta Lampert were apartment building owners seeking a new eastside property close-in. They wondered whether

---

[1] We use the term "partner" in two ways: to denote a shareolder in the Limited Liability Corporation owning the land ; and for individual owners in the Homeowners Association that was formed after construction.

we might be interested in a building in Portland's Central Eastside Industrial District. The location was not right for our project, with busy streets in a couplet north and south of the building, but they joined our quest. Jane Ediger also climbed aboard. She had worked for the Portland Development Commission and knew about pro formas.

Jane said we needed a "program." A small list of concepts would not get us far with a design firm or a lender. We needed detail on sizes of units, floor plans and more on construction materials. Web-surfing took us to new energy-efficient materials and construction techniques, popping up as fast as apps for a smart phone. Passive house construction was particularly intriguing with its tight 'envelope' so thick that heating and cooling needs would be reduced by 90 percent. This building method is called "passivehaus" in Europe (had to be cool), and thousands already existed in northern Europe although few had been built in the U.S. Our heads spun, but homework and meetings yielded our "program."[2]

Professional or Citizen Developer?

Caution suggested hiring an experienced developer to deal with architects, builders and subcontractors and to land a construction loan; but we'd bought, sold and remodeled homes, apartments and other buildings over the years. Our project would be relatively small, and developers charge substantial fees. A dangerous combination of overconfidence and do-it-yourself instincts led us to delay the decision to engage a developer.

---

[2] See https://ankenyrow.wordpress.com/ for our intiial program.

Required Skills

Architect/Design: *to develop conceptual drawings, schematics, and construction drawings.*

Bookkeeper/Accountant: *to track finances for the group and prepare tax filings and specialized analyses such as reserve studies.*

Real Estate Agent: *to help you find and acquire a site which meets your needs.*

Contractor: *with the skill to build the actual project.*

Financial Advisor: *to assist in obtaining financing, if necessary.*

Group Facilitator: *to help a group of "citizen developers" make decisions.*

Lawyer: *to provide specialized legal expertise to meet state condo or coop law.*

Operating Manager: *to coordinate the ownership group and their interface with the contractor and experts.*

Owner Representative: *to supervise contractors and subcontractors on behalf of the owner.*

There are three basic choices for building a project such as we envisioned, spanning a spectrum from a total, do-it-yourself approach covering all requisite skills (highly unlikely) to total outsourcing for all necessary expertise (a developer or development corporation).

Most "citizen developers," who are building for themselves, will end somewhere in the middle; they will possess some but not all the skills. They will need to assemble an appropriate team and create some legal structure: Limited Liability Corporation (LLC), partnership, etc.

A developer, whether an individual, partnership, or a corporation, will be expected to have or to provide all the necessary skills; and they will receive a premium for their role. We opted to be our own developer. After all, several of us were lawyers. The other partners raised their eyebrows, but trusted the lawyers to know when to turn to an attorney actually practicing real estate law. The lawyer members experimented with legal documents found at websites.

Finding the Site

We were now seven people– anxious to get going. It was 2006 and we weren't getting any younger. We engaged a broker but were unready for Bernie. He had kinetic energy to spare and sent waves of prospects our way.

Bernie disregarded our criteria and sent potential locations he liked. We sent posses to check them out and issued regular rejection slips. One day, we examined a 10,000 square foot parcel in the Irvington neighborhood of NE Portland. There was an existing 10-unit apartment on the site, 1970s vintage, just as lovely as most of the buildings of that era. The broker acknowledged it was not what we were looking for, but he suggested it would allow us to get in the game. We could always do a "1031 Exchange"[3] later.

The site met some of our criteria. The "Walkscore," a measure of destinations within walking distance from grocery stores to child-care, was a solid 78. In January, 2008, after weeks of wrangling, we became owners of the Regal Terrace Apartments.

We drafted documents to create "Tillamook LLC." This process introduced us to the challenges of gaining agreement from seven people. Without plenty of time and good food and drink, we might never have progressed beyond draft documents. We met frequently and talked endlessly but fruitfully. We filed the partnership documents and turned to design.

Little did we know that the Great Recession was unfolding. Fortunately, we had purchased property which generated income. Developers holding vacant parcels began to tumble all around us.

---

[3] Section 1031 of the Internal Revenue Code allows one to defer payment of capital gains tax when you sell business or investment property if you reinvest the proceeds in similar property through a like-kind exchange.

SOLARC Design

Research for a firm oriented to sustainability led us to SOLARC of Eugene, which we paid for a design based on our program. Their concept showed three detached buildings connected by causeways around a central courtyard in a "U" shape facing the street. Each building had four stories of stacked one-floor condos. There was plenty of light to each unit and a few tuck-under parking spots. Although the design was appealing, a preliminary estimate of construction costs was high. We hit the pause button.

The Recession rendered the Tillamook idea academic. The glut of condos on the market became obvious. Some of us refused to acknowledge reality until a visit to a representative of Umpqua Bank. He showed us a spreadsheet comparing the 2007 asking prices of comparable condos with the 2009 auction prices. The units were selling for $150,000 less per condo than the SOLARC unit construction cost.

The partners held a last project meeting and decided it was over. We were fortunate to break even on this venture and resolved to be more careful in the future. We licked our wounds and went home.

Resuming the Search

An uptick in the economy in the summer of 2010 spawned a conversation among the original partners: Dick, Lavinia, Michael and Francie. We would attempt the co-housing, aging- in-place, "green" concept on a smaller scale.

Site Selection

Criteria for Site: Target neighborhoods; vacant lot or built space; walkability; local amenties desired; mass transit; site size and orientation for solar; cost.

Program: Details on unit sizes, floor plans, and basic construction materials

Financial Capabilities: How are you going to finance the design phase and the construction phase? Home equity loan ? Construction loan?

We re-started the search: this time for a plot a quarter-mile from our favorite eastside grocery stores. The elements of our initial program remained our criteria.

Lavinia's daughter spotted a vacant 6,500 square foot parcel for sale in the heart of the neighborhood that had appealed to us earlier. The lot was four blocks from a good grocery. A neighborhood theater – $3 movies for seniors – was three blocks away.

Eighteen restaurants and a choice of cafes lay within a six block radius. WalkScore called the area a "Walking Paradise" with a Walk Score of 92. The location was also designated a "Biker's Paradise," achieving an amazing Bike Score of 98.

Project Site

The parcel had 65 feet of unobstructed southern exposure for solar and was 100 feet deep with the most flexible zoning in the city's code (Commercial/Mixed Use). We could build to 45 feet, needed no onsite parking and could construct more units than were in our program, a near-perfect match with our wish list. We envisioned three townhouses, recognizing it might be a stretch to call co-housing, but our destinies had not yet played out. The asking price was $370,000, but recession was strong. We offered $305,000. The owner and his bank (because the property was "over-leveraged") accepted, and in August, 2010, we began due diligence, a tortuous, anxiety-ridden, four-month "discovery tour".

Each week turned up new problems. A light access easement existed in favor of the owner building apartments to our west. There was an easement in favor of the city for a sewer connection to the street from the adjacent 6,100 square foot parcel immediately to the east on which stood a vacant and decrepit industrial building owned by the same owner as the tract for which we negotiated. We decided to live with the light easement; the apartment developer seemed quite reasonable in the event we might want to modify it. A sharp elbow from the broker persuaded the owner to resolve the sewer easement.

Our due diligence included an environmental survey. We did a "level one" survey, which involved review of city records for underground tanks, pipelines and possible contamination. No digging was required, and no problems were discovered. We thought there were none.

We had rounded the final turn when the broker called with news of a third easement: 10 feet wide and 100 feet deep - one sixth of our site - to allow fire access to the old industrial building to the east. We told the owner to get the easement removed or the deal would fall apart. That could happen, he said, only if the building was demolished, and he intended to remodel it for small food spaces.

A smoldering group of partners held a dinner wake to discuss where to look next. A bottle of wine in, Michael proposed a rash solution. Another bottle and we embraced the concept: we would buy the second parcel and demolish the building ourselves. The two parcels if joined, we reasoned, would be more valuable without the building. We could build a more robust version of our co-housing concept on what would now be a 12,600 square foot site, or we could build apartments to rent on the east parcel to sustain us in the golden years. If we lost our steam, we could always sell the east parcel for a nice gain when the recession ended. We offered the same price/square foot we'd offered for the first parcel. Two days later we were sobered by news the owner and bank agreed to our price.

With mild trepidation, we started due diligence on the second lot. We feared nuclear waste or leaking storage tanks under the old industrial building. Surprisingly, the environmental review gave the site a nearly a clean bill of health. There was asbestos in the floor tile of a bathroom, but this could be removed prior to demolition without great cost. After five months of anxiety, we closed the deal at the end of 2010 and became owners of the two parcels. We would build five to seven units. We worried about how long it would take to make decisions if we had seven homes (as many as 14 partners) involved in decision-making. It had been slow going with only seven people, testing our reserves of patience. We'd been talking about this since 2005; we'd been aging in place alright. We were in a hurry, but we didn't want to under-build the site.

Demolition

We celebrated the dawning of 2011 with no sense of loss as we demolished the empty warehouse; the building was ugly and had no history worth remembering.

No one objected or cared. The city lifted the fire easement May 20.

Going Design-Build

We did not know what "design-build" meant when we chose SOLARC to produce the Tillamook conceptual design, but that brief experience gave us pause once we realized the result was far outside our budget. We had not given them a budget because we did not want to confine creativity, but now we knew better.

We revised our "program" to fit the Ankeny site and worked up a budget for the project. Preparing more detailed financials again raised the "developer" question, which we had not progressed far enough in our Tillamook effort to resolve. Now we were a bit more seasoned and had a clearer concept for the project: six or seven units rather than 10 to 15.

Building without a developer would save money. We considered the risks but continued our record of overconfidence.

Considerations for Citizen Developers

	Pros	Cons
Developer	Broad Expertise, Coordination of functions	5 to 10% additional cost; many decisions made by developer as opposed to owners
Do It Yourself	No developer overhead	Expertise gaps
Hybrid	Owner group, not developer, leads	Need to ensure availability and coordination of required skills

We had bought and sold many houses, managed rentals, owned a commercial building and were lawyers and planners. Our hope was to tell our partner-prospects they would get their units at cost without a developer's fee and to assure people in the neighborhood that we were not developers, but rather building homes for ourselves.

We consulted the web and friends to chose firms to interview. This search introduced us to the design-build model, which seemed straightforward. Rather than have an architect design the project and then take the design to a builder, an architect would design with a builder in the same firm, checking for cost and practicality. A creative and innovative architect might propose a fabulously beautiful facade; the builder could point out it would cost a fortune. The architect might suggest a scupper to receive rainwater from the roof and pour over the edge in an eye-catching waterfall; the builder might point out it would freeze in cold weather and pose a hazard to foot traffic. Design-build would mean architects and builders on the same team from the first meeting until the last nail was driven home.

Instinct told us design-build would be crucial if we intended to be our own developers. We would be parties to the back-and-forth between the design and construction sides, learning more and inserting our interests with information from both, but we reserved judgment pending interviews.

We interviewed nine firms– architectural and design-build companies– exhibiting differences in vision, style and creativity. We selected three and engaged each in a design competition based on our program. "Pay them a modest fee so they take you and the competition seriously," Dick's brother, a LEED architect, advised.

We paid the three firms $1,500 each to take us through a design charrette and present us with a concept at a follow-up meeting. Two were design-build, and builders on their team participated in the meetings. The third was an architectural firm. Ironically (and we took note), this company emphasized it would partner with one of the two design-build companies. This reinforced our expectation that design and construction would be better if integrated.

Choosing Green Hammer

Green Hammer had built or played a design or modeling role in most of the passive houses constructed in Oregon. The owner taught courses in passive house construction and efficient design. Their architect had published on Passive House (PH) modeling and construction.

We chose Green Hammer to reap the rewards of the design-build model. Two or three "extra" people from the build side at design meetings would add to cost, but we believed the gain from avoiding miscommunication in the back-and-forth between architect and building contractor would more than compensate for the small cost.

There were rewards, especially in the design development stage, as we refined our schematic design. The build side found significant savings, keeping us within shouting distance of our budget. Green Hammer adjusted the size and placement of windows, for example, reducing cost without jeopardizing achievement of passive house standards or net zero. The build side also persuaded us to change materials from stucco to Hardie board for siding, resulting in substantial savings.

Our "schematic design" progressed to a point of sufficient detail to show potential partners a site plan, facades, elevations, floor plans and a reliable budget. With as many as seven units and fourteen partners, we realized we needed strong coordination with the design-build team. One essential is a "strong force" representing the owners that pushes the design and build sides to communicate regularly and reach decisions. Another essential is to ensure subcontractors, such as landscape designers, are integrated with the design-build team. Paying close attention to these prescriptions can keep cost overruns in check and reduce chances for mistakes on the ground.

The partners chose Lavinia as "Operating Manager" and principal link to Green Hammer. Fortunately, she recognized the need to shore up some weak spots in our combined expertise. On her recommendation, we hired Jessy Olson, an experienced architect and developer, on an hourly basis to come to our aid at important junctures as an "owner representative." It was a very good decision.

Despite challenges faced by Green Hammer and the ownership group, we remain convinced the design-build model worked well for us.

CHAPTER 2: Shooting for Net Zero

Before we had put our first concept on paper, we sought advice from Mike O'Brien, Portland's green building expert, a long-time friend generous with his time and passionate about his work. "How can we build green?" we asked. He answered with a primer on energy conservation. First, chose your building site with energy efficiency in mind. Second, reduce your demand for energy. Third, produce as much of your electricity demand as you can.

1. The Site

We'd taken great care selecting our site. We'd chosen a site in a close-in, walkable neighborhood, which would dramatically reduce our transportation carbon footprints. Our expert friend said, "You are well on your way to smaller footprints; now, on to energy efficiency. Your site has excellent solar access." Photovoltaic (PV) technology, he said, was advancing rapidly, and panel prices were dropping. "If you insulate well and install the right number of panels, you will generate more electricity than you need. That is, you can get to 'net zero'."

2. Reducing Demand

We had stumbled onto "passivhaus" (PH) on the internet while searching for energy-efficient construction materials. The essence of PH is a tight, well-insulated building envelope. It was developed in Germany in the last quarter of the 20th century to reduce energy demand. At the time we initiated our project, it was the fastest growing energy-efficient housing construction technique. There are now hundreds of thousands of passive houses in Europe. Those built to standards have proven good on the promise: a 90 percent reduction in heating and cooling electricity.

We imagined small houses built like bunkers with which older Europeans are quite familiar. We contemplated privations - small windows and Jimmy Carter cardigans. But further research turned up a PH website that featured a 2,400 square foot craftsman bungalow with a hair dryer superimposed. The message was not subtle: "You can heat this baby with an appliance!" Another site suggested reliance upon body heat from regular dinner parties.

When we interviewed design firms for our project, we asked about PH. One firm firmly opposed it: "You can't open the windows!" We dropped that firm from further consideration. Several others were lukewarm: "PH is overkill in the northwest's moderate climate." Noting that our climate is much like Germany's, and the Germans are so very serious, we discounted this advice.

We were already leaning toward the design-build model. Green Hammer's PH experience and enthusiasm for it set the hook. Early design sessions only strengthened our resolve to build to PH standards.

Elements of Passive House Construction

Airtight Building Construction	Mechanical Air Filtration	Quality Indoor Air Comfortable Heat Reduced Air Infiltration	
Super Insulation/Extra Thick Walls	No Central Heating Required	Minimal Heat & AC Needs Stable Indoor Temperature Sound Insulation	
Eliminate Thermal Bridging	Stop Heat and Cooling Loss	Even and Stable Heat	
High Performance Windows	Reduced Heat Loss & Air Leakage	Avoidance of cold spots	
Energy Efficiency	Only Minimal Heating/AC Needed, if any	Reduced Energy Bills	

It helped that Socrates was a fan of south-facing housing with verandas to shield from the sun during the summer and to trap warmth in winter when the sun hangs low. PH envelopes lose little heat in winter or cooling in summer because of prodigious insulation in the walls and ceilings, a slab poured into a bed of rigid foam, triple-pane windows and doors that might work in submarines, and a Heat Recovery Ventilator (HRV) that circulates air throughout the house eight times a day and captures 93 percent of the heat from air exhausted to the outside. The energy savings were in the building itself, not in systems with short life-spans and whose manufacturers tended—like car-builders – to over-promise savings.

We embarked upon the road to "net zero." PH would dramatically reduce our electricity needs; the PV panels would generate as much or more electricity than we needed for appliances and devices. We were only vaguely aware of additional considerations that would flow from our PH decision. GH architect Dylan Lamar, tongue firmly in cheek, plunged us into the basics of PH design and construction. "Every window, every door is a concession. Every vent is a failure of imagination." He got our attention.

Sealing the Envelope

Slab Insulation

From design we turned to the building envelope. GH proudly showed us how they would "wrap" our living spaces. First, they would sink the concrete slab in a bed of foam insulation strong enough to support bridge pilings, and as a bonus, absorb some of an earthquake's shock.

We tried to imagine the slab comfortably resting on foam. When the construction crew "made" the bed, we rubbed our eyes in disbelief. The crew placed big chunks of white foam - 16 inches thick - in trenches they dug and poured the slab and footings directly onto the foam.

Zola Window

PH's double-wall construction can accommodate enough cellulose to reach R-46. And PH requires thermal breaks in the walls to eliminate "thermal bridging", the unwanted conduction of heated or cooled air through wall studs to the outside. The cellulose in the ceiling would achieve R-102, far exceeding the city's leading-edge code requirements.

The Zola windows and doors imported from Poland dazzled us. These are windows and doors with gravitas! They are three and a half inches thick and encased in beautiful Maranti wood trim. Triple-paned with gas between panes, they deliver an R-factor of 8.1 The windows tilt or turn for ventilation flexibility. We wanted to use windows and doors manufactured in the

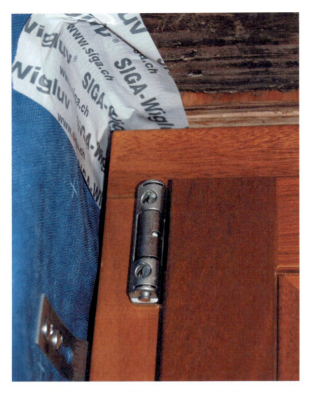

SIGA Wrap & Tape behind Door

U.S., but there were none of Zola's quality at the time we ordered. U.S. companies are now closing in. GH had told us the walls had to be "tight" to meet PH standards. SIGA Wigluv tape sealed the wall spaces between door and window openings. Then the walls and facades were covered by SIGA membrane.

A subcontractor of Energy Trust of Oregon conducted two PH-required pressure tests several months apart. A crew pressurized the living space as though it were a balloon and searched for leaks. Twice, they found none. Interior walls were ready for sheetrock and the exteriors for plywood sheathing. We thought that was it, but

the exterior walls had something else coming: ¾-inch DensGlass sheathing went over the membranes. Only then would the siding go on. All in all, exterior walls measured just under 16 inches thick.

We were in awe.

Wall Cutaway

PH Construction

For the envelope to be thermally tight, there could not be too many doors, windows or vents, especially on the north side. There would have to be an opening for the Heat Recovery Ventilator (HRV), of course, to ensure introduction of fresh air and venting of stale air from the airtight living space; but any others were frowned upon.

We saw where this was going. Gas stovetops vent to the outside. So do clothes dryers, gas fireplaces, and hood vents over stovetops. What of these "essential" openings?

We took a stand: "No condensing dryers!" We'd experienced those 'dryers' in Europe. A three-hour cycle resulted in laundry only 80 percent dry. Never again would we don damp clothing!

Architect Dylan Lamar flashed us an unsympathetic grin. "How about the time-honored drying technique of southern Europe: hang the laundry across the courtyard!" He invoked mothers leaning out of third-story windows to drape clothes from lines stretching across the piazza. The notion was more pleasant than memories of French condensing dryers. But that image faded quickly; we live in the rainy Northwest. Dylan had another idea. "We can build you a small shed in the courtyard for a washer and conventional dryer that partners could share!" That idea inspired no favorable images. We refused to yield courtyard space.

Dylan offered up one additional thought, to install condensing dryers and devote a little interior floor space to a "drying room" where we could hang near-dry laundry for finishing. But that floor space would take a chunk from our coveted great rooms.

Further research revealed condensing dryer technology had improved. Green Hammer owner Stephen Aiguier installed one in his home and reported fully-dry clothes. Reluctantly, we embraced condensing dryers.

Spirits fell another notch when we realized we could not have natural gas fireplaces because they produce toxic gases that are particularly dangerous in a tight house. Green Hammer suggested ethanol fireplaces. No venting is necessary because ethanol is a biofuel and breaks down into water and CO_2 without toxic residual. Ethanol is expensive, but some partners were ready to pay for dancing flames in a firebox on cold winter nights. As a bonus, in the event of an electricity blackout, heat from the ethanol fireplace could maintain some warmth in the passive house.

In our previous homes, we had cooked with gas, which offered precise control and quick delivery of heat. Still, reduction of fossil fuel use was our highest priority, and we knew nitrogen dioxide, carbon monoxide, particulate, hydrocarbons, VOCs and other chemicals are released when cooking with gas. Reversion to electric stovetops struck us as atavistic; we'd missed the movement to induction stovetops among chefs. Induction stoves cook with electromagnetism, now highly energy efficient. Only forty percent of energy in gas is used when cooking; with induction, 84 percent is utilized. Induction ranges provide better heat control than gas and are much easier to clean.

A bonus of induction stovetops is that only the bottom of the pan on the "burner" gets hot. If you touch the stovetop, you will not be singed; bodies are not magnetic. Aging became a little less hazardous. The small downside was the need to replace copper, aluminum or other non-magnetic cookware. We took another step into the future.

Recirculating range hoods would be required. We imagined smoke from searing halibut tearing our eyes and clouding the great room. Green Hammer told us the HRVs would take care of this problem and sensed it was time for a full lesson on the HRVs.

Heat Recovery Ventilators

Heat Recovery Ventilator

Our HRVs were manufactured by Zender of Switzerland. Once again, no HRV made in the U.S. at the time we placed orders could achieve the Zender's efficiency.

The hardware would be installed in a closet with a pump to draw in fresh air and to exhaust stale air through five-inch flexible tubing in the ceilings of each room. The HRV would run constantly and change air in each unit the equivalent of eight times a day. Each room has a ceiling intake and exhaust, and the HRV does additional duty as the bathroom ventilator.

The Zenders have four basic settings, including low for long absences and high for parties and shamefully long showers. "High" also serves for ventilation for high-temperature cooking. With both range hood and HRV set to high, the exhaust vent for the HRV would inhale the residual smoke and send it "away."

Piping for Air Distribution

Tight buildings can accumulate toxics embedded in materials and furnishings, despite superior ventilation. Green Hammer helped us choose building materials, such as paint and finishes with no or very low volatile organic compounds (VOCs). We did the same with rugs, upholstery and other furnishings. All our wood was Forest Stewardship Council (FSC)-certified, which ensures responsible forest management to promote "environmentally appropriate, socially beneficial and economically viable management of the world's forests."

Commissioning

Naval shipbuilders don't simply launch a ship and give the captain the keys. The ship must be "commissioned!" Shipbuilders take the crew on a months-long shakedown cruise to ensure correct operation. Before Ankeny Row partners took the controls of their homes, Green Hammer took us through "building commissioning." The buildings, they told us, would deliver the promised energy efficiency only if we operated them properly. After our shakedown cruise (only three hours), they distributed operating manuals — hard and electronic copies — that included a schedule for cleaning and replacing all manner of filters, valves and batteries. We learned about 'minding the mass.' We abandoned an old value of turning heat way down when we left for a trip. Green Hammer said we would burn more electricity if we let the units get too cold or too hot. Proper operation of windows and fans and setting thermostats to the right range would save electricity and keep us more comfortable.

Underappreciated Bonuses of PH

Our indoor air quality would be the best we had ever experienced. HRV filters would remove most particulates. Mold would likely be unknown to us, as would stale air. If we suffered from allergies, we'd have some relief. We would feel no drafts from cold pockets near the windows or doors.

Then, there's the silence of living in a passive house. The "thunk" that followed each closing of the new Zola doors and windows was a satisfying reminder that 16-inch walls with R-46 insulation, ceilings with R-102, and triple-paned windows and doors would bring a quiet none of us had experienced in any prior home.

Passive House and Earth Advantage Certifications

Having embarked upon passive house construction, we wanted the Passive House Institute of the U.S. (PHIUS) to recognize our accomplishment. We assumed Green Hammer would assiduously take us to or beyond PHIUS standards. But during our first budget trimming exercise ("value engineering"), we learned that there are many independent programs to encourage energy efficiency and environmental responsibility, each with its own certification system. We wanted to ring every bell we could. Then Green Hammer explained how detailed they are, how much costly time they would have to invest in the effort, and the fees associated each certification. We decided to build to PH standards, but not seek PHIUS certification. Instead, we would focus on the Earth Advantage system and seek its certification. It was the most comprehensive program and, hence, would account for all our efficiency and environmental efforts, from passive solar to low or no VOCs inside our units. Upon completion Ankeny Row earned Earth Advantage's Platinum and Net Zero Ready certifications.

PH brought us a long way toward net zero. Now it was time to close the energy gap. We moved to the demand side. Our appliance choices would make a big difference.

Tame the Appliances

Heating and cooling systems (HVAC) typically consume 40 percent of total household energy needs. Did we even need a HVAC system in our passive houses? Could we rely upon our dryers, ovens and regular dinner parties if we needed more heat than solar radiation gave us? The city's building code rendered these questions moot: the code requires a heating system in all new residences.

Mini-Split Heat Pump

We installed a single mini-split in each home connected to an external air-to-air heat pump. Minis are highly efficient, known to cut electricity use 50 percent below other electric resistance systems (furnaces or baseboards, for example) due to the absence of duct systems that lose as much as 30 percent of energy; and they transfer heat or cooling from the air rather than generate heat enabling them to provide heating for much less than the cost of conventional systems.

MiniSplit Compressor

They would also serve as air conditioners, all while de-humidifying better.

Water heating is number two in household energy demand. We chose GE GeoSpring heat-pump water heaters. They use electricity for running pumps and fans, but for heating the water heat is extracted from the outside air. That means they use only 25 percent of electricity used by standard electric water heaters.[4]

We paid more for such high efficiency appliances, but rebates and tax credits resulted in rapid recoupment of the additional cost.

With Green Hammer we developed a "base" package for kitchen and laundry appliances (fridge, range or stovetop and oven, microwave, kitchen hood, dishwasher, washer and dryer) with a budget of $8,400 per home. We channeled our passion to reach net zero into a mad chase to beat Energy Star. We shared charts and tables on energy usage. U.S. Department of Energy spreadsheets showed all models of manufacturers of the big energy users among appliances sold in the U.S. There were thousands to choose from. Appliance madness! But we made our choices, often spending more for higher-than-Energy Star efficiency.

---

4 http://www.qualitysmith.com/request/article/heat-pump-vs-electric-heat/

3. Make Your Own Energy: The Rest of the Way to Net Zero

The flip side of demand is energy generation. We quickly settled on passive solar radiation and active photovoltaic solar generation as our energy sources.

Passive Solar: The Easy Energy

Solar radiation comes first. We had 126 feet of unobstructed southern exposure along Ankeny Street. Correct orientation of buildings is critical. It was obvious for us as our property runs length-wise almost perfectly east-west: the houses would face south.

How to shape the buildings presented us with conflicting priorities. We favored gabled roofs, which we had loved on our existing homes and are common in the neighborhoods around our site. We wanted our buildings to fit in. Also, it would be easy to mount panels on the south slope of roofs on all three buildings. The first concept plan drawn by GH had gabled roofs.

Modeling changed our thinking. In the "shoulder" seasons— spring and fall—gables on the homes fronting on Ankeny Street would cast shadows on the courtyard and first-floor windows of the rear units. These shadows would reduce radiation to the rear units and shorten the growing season for the vegetable garden planned for the courtyard. In addition, gabled roofs on the front units sloped down on the south side, which reduced window space and, hence, solar radiation into those units.

We had to choose between our aesthetic and neighborhood compatibility and maximization of solar radiation to the units. Achieving net zero was a priority, and the choice was easier than we'd thought. We abandoned the gabled roof in favor of solar gain.

Placement of windows on homes without gables became more straightforward: more on the south side to heat the mass of the building; fewer on the north to reduce heat loss. Modeling told us how far to extend the eaves over the southern windows to reduce overheating. Green Hammer added generous south-facing decks on the second floors to supplement the eaves.

We rejected passive solar hot water heating. It would have required installation of another mechanical system and is less efficient than PV generation of the needed electricity.

Our choice to build to PH standards significantly affected the design of our buildings, and good design choices increased chances of getting to net zero.

Active Solar

Green Hammer determined the PV generation we would need to meet average electricity demand of our three-bedroom homes. They calculated each unit would need 13 PV panels (the common room required only six). This raised doubts among us because two of the three bedrooms in each home would serve principally as studies. They checked actual usage from two partners' existing homes and concluded demand may have been overestimated. With some irony, the matter was settled during the painful "value engineering" process (euphemism for chopping off project limbs) to staunch budget hemorrhaging.

We had chosen metal roofing for aesthetics and to keep maintenance costs (and condo fees) down, but faced with unpleasant choices, we were prepared to forsake metal for cheaper composite asphalt. Green Hammer informed us, however, that solar panels could easily snap onto a metal roof, which would make installation cheaper than if a structure to hold the panels was required. Clipping the panels to metal also eliminated the possibility of damage to the thermal shield by drilling holes in composite roofing. We happily resurrected metal roofing and instead decided to cut panels to 12 per unit. We could add panels later if necessary. As it turned out, 12 panels per unit did the job.

Solar Panels

Synchro Solar installed 24 kW generation – 78 panels in all - on the metal roof of the rear building. Twelve panels with 3.94 kW of generating capacity were allocated to each house and six to the common room. Each home would establish a "net metering" account with our electric utility, Portland General Electric (PGE). Solar panel-generated electricity flowed to the grid. PGE would report each home's use and generation monthly. At the end of the year, we would pay for electricity drawn from the grid in excess of generation, if any. By state law, PGE would pass excess generation to low-income households in its territory.

The Coveted Tax Credits

Initial partners were aware of tax credits and intended to pursue them. But we were focused on our overall goals and would have proceeded even if they'd not existed. Energy Trust of Oregon and the rising cost of our units sharpened our attention to tax credits. It seemed there was a credit for every efficiency measure we took, from photovoltaic solar panels to PH itself.

SynchroSolar said each owner would get a $6,000 state tax credit and a $3,000-4,000 federal tax credit for the 12 panels metered to its unit. They confirmed that panels must be owned by the person seeking the tax credit. (This raised an issue for partners because the panels would be atop the roof, ultimately owned by the homeowners association: see Chapter 6, Documents, Documents). The total cost of each unit's 12 panels was $17,833, including installation. In the end, each owner earned $6,000 of credit against Oregon taxes and $5,350 against federal taxes. These credits represented a subsidy of about 63 percent of the cost of the systems. The credits, together with the falling prices of panels, provide a very significant incentive, reflected in the spike in installation for residential use.

Each house received a state tax credit for the passive heat coming through our triple-pane windows for storage in the mass. The overall efficiency of our units' triple-pane windows and doors; insulation far exceeding code; water heater; HRV; and appliances—earned another credit ($5,000/unit) from Energy Trust of Oregon.

Our passive houses have no central heating; a unit's heating and cooling is provided by a single ductless air-source heat pump (mini-split). These systems earned a state credit worth 30 percent of the equipment cost.

An essential appliance in a passive house is the heat recovery ventilator (HRV). Our Zehnder HRVs run continuously and change the air in the houses the equivalent of eight times a day. They filter the outside air drawn into the house and cool or heat by transfer of temperature from exhaust or intake air. The state tax credit covered approximately 10 percent of the installed cost.

The cumulative value of all the credits came to $19,601, three percent of the base cost of our townhouse units.

Besides our desire to occupy our homes as soon as possible, there was little we looked forward to more than word from PGE that we had succeeded in achieving net zero in our first year.

Chapter 3: Aging in Place

Aging in Place[5] signifies different things to different people, but for us, it meant fashioning a more dignified living situation for our seventies, eighties, and, with luck, nineties than had been enjoyed by some of our parents and older friends. "My mom and dad were looking for something like this as they got older," Dave Siegel, the first new partner to join the project with his wife Lainie Smith, said "but there was not enough on the market so they ended up in an assisted living complex with 1400 other people."

As they looked back after living at Ankeny Row for the first year, Dave and Lainie summarized: "For many years, we were part of a group of four couples. We had dinners together, travelled to foreign countries, and during wine-fueled evenings would ask each other, 'What are we going to do when we grow up?' We talked about living together, but it never came together, life threw up too many distractions. When we got an email from Dick about the project, we were very interested." Lainie added: "A garden! And easy access to outdoor spaces." The decision to live at Ankeny Row was not only a question about the ability to stay in one's house as one aged but also one of quality of life.

The key, beyond design, is location in a walkable neighborhood, full access to a first floor where one could comfortably live, and the easy availability of non-car transportation. There is developing science in this area as Baby Boomers retire in wave after wave.[6]

---

[5] The CDC defines aging in place as 'the ability to live in one's own home and community, independently, and comfortably regardless of age, income, or activity level." https://en.wikipedia.org/wiki/Aging_in_place

[6] Links to suggested reading on aging in place. http://aginginplacepublications.com/product-category/aging-in-place/

Aging changes us all and, to a varying degree and at different times, brings about some or all of the following: reduced mental capability, vision, hearing, muscle strength and mobility, and increased risk of illness. Obviously genetics, healthy eating, exercise and many other factors also impact physical faculties, but the choice of where we live and how we design our homes can make a huge difference in our ability to cope with diminishments.

Much of what is discussed in this chapter applies equally to our other goals of energy efficiency and intentional community. Co-housing assists with the needs of aging through the proximity and friendships facilitated by such integrated housing. Walkable communities and ease of non-car transportation are relevant to energy sustainability goals as well as aging. Induction stove tops and ethanol fireplaces are efficient but also safer.

Social isolation is one of the great dangers of aging. Shared entertainment such as yoga in our common room and a common TV serve not only aging but also the creation of community; and close proximity and involvement in a common Homeowner's Association (HOA) with friends and neighbors means more social interaction and the opportunity to assist each other to maintain a long-term "angle of repose."

Location

In our search for a project site, we settled on southeast Portland because of its density, diversity, and relative affordability, and we established a radius of two miles from the center of the downtown to ensure proximity to cultural amenities there. Location is central.

> **Walkability**
>
> - A Center: a focal point or main street
> - Density: sufficient people to support retail businesses
> - Parks and public spaces
> - Affordable housing: to ensure diversity
> - Pedestrian-friendly Design: buildings close to the street and parking in back
> - Diverse transportation options: public transport, bicycles, pedestrians
> - Wide-range of Retail: close enough that one can walk most places

The more you walk and the less you use motorized transport, the more sustainable and healthy your life style. As we get older, our world shrinks, making a rich diversity of walkable destinations even more desirable. On foot, we are more likely to interact with neighbors while engaged in daily life.

Walkability[7] is one of those fancy concepts, such as charrette, which some of us had never heard before but learned in the process of designing Ankeny Row. Buckman neighborhood, where Ankeny Row is located, has a walkability score of 92,[8] which is very high. Many aspects of walkability are determined by macro-planning such as urban density, zoning, street life, public transportation and curb cuts.[9]

Within a three block radius of Ankeny Row, we have grocery shopping, Da Vinci Arts middle school, Central Catholic high school, a movie theater, a dentist, Zoom emergency care, a barber and hair salon, massage center, a brewery, two wine shops, four coffee houses (it is after all Portland), ten restaurants, furniture stores, car repair, veterinarian, park for dogs, and frequent bus service. Within a ten block radius, we have a hospital and numerous medical specialists, Buckman grade school, several gyms, live music venues, four more full service grocery stores, the epicenter of the Portland restaurant scene, Laurelhurst, one of Portland's most beautiful parks, and additional public transit service.

---

[7] Wikipedia, https://en.wikipedia.org/wiki/Walkability;

[8] On 4/28/16, www.walkscore.com rated our area as 92, a walker's paradise, good for public transit, and at 98 "Biker's Paradise."

[9] http://www.walkable.org/

Transportation

The availability of numerous transportation options was also a key parameter in our search for a new home. Ankeny Row is located one block from the #20 bus, which shoots us to the northern part of downtown in ten minutes, from door to Powell's Books, one of the great literary shrines of Portland, or to the Living Room Theater, where you can have dinner while watching indie movies. Portland's growing mass transit system of buses, light rail and streetcars provides good access to downtown, all four quadrants of the city core, and to the airport light rail line. Ankeny Street is one of southeast Portland's major bicycle arterials.

Bike Room

Our bike room of 150 sf is tucked behind the common room and provides one bike spot for each of the 11 members of our community and a bike bollard out front for guests. Sharing such a facility has meant we share bike tools and racks, as well as giving ourselves more space in our home units. Our fall back plan is to progress from road bike to fat tire bikes, fat tires to three wheelers or electric-assisted bicycles…um, and then walking…slowly.

Public transport, along with bicycles, has meant that days go by without using our cars.

Design Features

Green Hammer walked us through design features involved in accommodating the needs of aging-in-place, the most important of which is access. All five of our two-story homes were built to be accessible from the street level with home entrances without steps and barrier-free entrances to the common room, the bike room, storage units and garden shed. The passages around kitchen islands and into rooms accept wheel chairs. Bathroom counters, walk in showers and toilet seats met Americans with Disabilities Act (ADA) specifications, and lever-door handles rather than knobs for all doors, lighting at foot level on steps,[10] and cabinet and drawer pulls follow ADA-design recommendations.

Most important, each unit has what realtors call "master-on-main:" a bedroom and bathroom on first floors so owners, if needed, can live in their homes without climbing stairs. We realized that with eleven older adults, one or more might become wheelchair-bound or unable to climb stairs, and we built master bedrooms on the first floor.

Drawing by Daryl Rantis, Lead Architect for Green Hammer

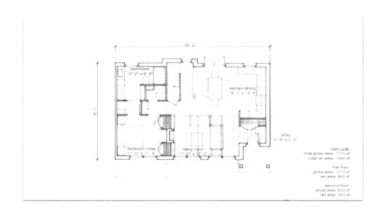

First Floor, Front Unit

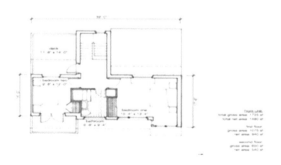

Second Floor, Front Unit

10 http://gero.usc.edu/nrcshhm/aboutus/#whatis

If anyone were to become disabled, he or she could live on the first floor with a master bathroom and all the comforts of a one-bedroom condo. The second floor could be used for guests or a caretaker with a full bathroom, landing, porch and two bedrooms.

There were compromises, of course. The heights of kitchen islands were designed for cooks but too high for the wheel-chair bound. Under-counter cabinets in bathrooms were flush with the front edges of the counters for aesthetics and ease of cleaning; but this precludes wheel chairs from rolling close to the counters, a problem solved by retrofitting, if needed.

Physical disability would not force anyone to move. Aging-in-place is a balancing act requiring you to plan for future requirements while satisfying present aesthetic and physical space configuration needs.

CHAPTER 4: Living with Friends

Michael, Francie, Dick and Lavinia had been friends for years, travelling together and, at times, job sharing. Community was a core value to us and integral to other fundamental goals of environmental sustainability and housing compatible with the aging process. We searched for a site that would allow construction of a courtyard community and hired Green Hammer to design buildings to facilitate interaction among the residents while maintaining individual space and privacy.

The two couples paid costs from purchase and clearing of the land, through the hiring process for a potential architect and builder, to the development of a schematic design by Green Hammer with a detailed architectural rendering of the plan, one step short of construction drawings. We took no development fee because our goal from the start was to initiate and build a community that we would live in with others, not to make a profit from our effort. This was an important principle for the seven other partners who eventually joined. We would all be equal in decision-making and running of our project and eventually the Homeowner's Association.

Adding New Partners[11]

By January, 2012, we were ready to add new partners. We had an overall construction price from Green Hammer (the process to get there is discussed in Chapter 5). Based on the construction cost from Green Hammer, the cost of land, and reliance on outlandish assumptions,

---

[11] Brief biographies of the partners in Ankeny Row are available in Appendix 1.

our self-appointed "finance guy" Michael came up with a preliminary all-in price for the condo homes of $570,000[12] for the five two-floor condos and $350,000 for the second floor condo.

Initially, the two couples considered developing a list of criteria for additional partners for Ankeny Row. On advice from Eli Spivak, an experienced developer, they rejected this notion, however, as frustrating and ultimately ineffective because of numerous variables and decided to rely on thorough vetting of each potential prospect.

Both couples created a list of ten to fifteen close friends that might be interested and spread the word through friendship circles and by word-of-mouth. Although a clear concept existed and a rough approximation of cost, the decision to join and pay a refundable $10,000 deposit was still a leap of faith; newcomers were joining with us to build a project, not buying an already exiting home.

On January 19th, the Daily Journal of Commerce ran a first-page article on the project using our recently minted name, Ankeny Row, *"Empty nesters planning Southeast Portland housing development."* Dick was quoted modestly asserting, "Twenty-eighth (Avenue) and East Burnside (Street) is one of the most vital and lively nodes on the east side. I just think we found one of the best (neighborhoods)." With an eye toward luring in prospective partners, he added: "People used to flee to the suburbs and now …want to come back to centers where they can access transit, and walkable neighborhoods and services (are) within easy walking distance. We want to be able to walk and ride bikes."[13]

An online comment to this article by Mike O'Brien, Portland's green building expert, was euphoric. "This project exemplifies the future– as baby boomers retire and downsize they need less living space and more shared space. Owners will also share small cars. The goal is to reduce the footprint while enhancing livability. A very inspiring innovation!"

----

[12] By July 2015, a three bedroom house in the city of Portland had a median sale price of $345,000. Our houses were in a higher tier but cost less than the sale price for our existing homes.

[13] Read more: http://djcoregon.com/news/2012/01/19/empty-nesters-planning-southeast-portland-housing-development/#ixzz46gXrUJSr

---
Finding Partners

- *Expect curveballs*
- *Don't Panic*
- *Continue other tasks*
- *Be Flexible*

Despite our rising optimism, the first efforts were not a rousing success; the economy was still recovering from the Great Recession. Friends, who had been contemplating co-housing for years and had hoped to reserve a townhouse, were unable to make the leap because of the drop in home values.

By the second half of April, 2012, the partners had developed and released a "presentation packet," which explained the vision of the project, "passive house," and "net zero" and contained site plans and renderings, floor plans and elevations, "palette" selections for interior and exterior colors, the Schedule of Values and lists of optional finishes and furnishings. Also, a list of "Steps" had been borrowed from another co-housing project in Portland to inform people how they could join. Green Hammer created a link to the package at its website. Francie set up a blog as a second portal. Partners placed flyers with willing retailers near the site. We mowed the property and installed an attractive sign.

An open house at Green Hammer on the night of May 15th drew a respectable crowd of about 25. We showed slides, described Ankeny Row, and answered questions. Michael made a pitch from the partners. The following weeks were busy with emails, phone calls and coffees, tea, dinner, lunch or breakfast with prospective participants.

Lainie Smith and Dave Siegel were the first to join the new enterprise. Francie, Lavinia, and Dick had known them for a number of years in their workplaces and broader professional circles. Lainie and Dave chose the middle unit in the back row with impressive speed and determination. We were on our way but not yet close to the goal post.

A string of near misses made clear to us that a relatively passive approach to finding partners would be too slow for partners already "aging in place." Actual marketing was modest and the results disappointing. The partners began to entertain alternative plans. Should they turn one of the townhouses into two smaller stacked units? Build only four units on a portion of the tract and sell the balance? Or do a phased construction of the project as partners joined?

Before our imagination ran away with us, in May, Roger Chope and Anne Morrow, alerted to Ankeny Row by a friend, called out of the blue. They were not known to any of the three current couples in the LLC, but, of course, this being Portland, they were practically first cousins. Anne had worked with the husband of a life-time friend, and both Anne and Roger were in an Italian language group with another couple known to us for decades. With spies such as this, our due diligence was easy. They loved good food and tasty wines, they were politically progressive, and rode bikes like mad. Plus, Roger, an accountant, was oxymoronically funny. (As he made sure to point out, several of us as lawyers were, equally amazingly, quite honest). The deal was sealed with an excellent meal at their apartment in the Pearl.

Roger and Anne not only paid their deposit but brought another couple to the table, who unfortunately wanted an elevator to the one loft condo for their sunset years. Green Hammer said it would cost $30,000 for an elevator and reduce storage. Nonetheless, they made their deposit, bringing us to five, a whisper from a full house.

In September, a cousin of Michael and her spouse made a deposit on the last townhouse. They had been intrigued with the idea of co-housing and had lived in Portland before. We had reached the holy grail, but complacency was short-lived. The cousin could not commit to proceed with the project until their current house in Idaho sold. Their deposit was returned and we were one shy again.

By December, there were two other couples on a wait list for the fifth townhouse, which had been briefly reserved by the cousin. John and Carol Munson, one of the couples, had recently returned from a Peace Corps stint in Botswana, and Michael and Francie had known them for decades. Also, they were close friends and bridge partners to several other long-term friends. Again, the vetting process was easy. They evinced a healthy mix of enthusiasm, skepticism, seriousness and attention to detail. And all the other partners loved them.

"After retiring and selling the home in which we raised our family, John and I finished almost two years in the Peace Corps," Carol recalled. "We returned and searched for a new single family house….I wept at what we saw because nothing matched our idea of where we really wanted to live…then, in a universal synchronicity, we talked to a friend who mentioned Ankeny Row. We had breakfast with Francie and Dick and really liked the community concept."

Lavinia and Dick accompanied the Munsons to Green Hammer where they were walked through the drawings and sketch-up. The architect deftly changed the position and dimensions of the Unit 5 storage unit and showed them how it would look. John, the vegetable gardener, wondered why the roof over the loft was not "green." Green roofs unfortunately were a casualty of early budget trimming, but final details, Dick and Lavina explained, remained to be determined after all partners joined the LLC. The Munson made their deposit in mid-December, 2012.

What is achieved can also disappear like the morning mist. While we had been acquiring partners for unit number six, the couple who had a deposit in on the loft condo decided they could not proceed. It was time for some creative thought. The Smith/Siegels, Chope/Morrows, and Munsons had committed their deposit but not yet put in money to equalize everyone's financial contribution and make them partners in the LLC. Impatience struck again.

After some soul searching, we pasted together a route forward. We asked Stephen Aiguier, the President of Green Hammer, to become the owner of the last and smallest unit which remained; and he put in $40,000 as his initial capital contribution. The two initial couples lent him the money for the additional capital calls through construction at a four percent rate. In addition to allowing us to proceed, this also more closely aligned the owner and design/build point of view and eased some regulatory and insurance requirements. This whole framework was somewhat jerry-rigged and is described not as a model of investment efficiency but rather as example of the flexibility necessary to make this sort of project become a reality.

In the end, not every one of the first five couples knew all the others, but all were known by at least some of the other partners, often for as long as thirty years. "Knowing one of the other partners helped. You're taking a risk when you write a big check," Lainie had noted. Everyone bought into a common development scheme and cooperative process. The self-selection of this process resulted in many shared values.

"I work in the social sciences and think our community has worked amazingly well because we share common viewpoints," Sue Best, the last partner to join, commented. "We are a group of like-minded people willing to listen to each other. I'm the only partner who hadn't known any of the others before joining; I met with each of you to find out who you were before agreeing to join, and I know you vetted me in the same way."

Ankeny Rowers tend to be progressive, avid readers, bicyclists, wine and beer drinkers, dedicated cooks, gardeners, and frequent travelers. There was no litmus test, but like tends to draw like.

There was an interesting discussion around future sale of the houses by any of the original owners. To introduce too many restrictions into our Bylaws would be contrary to our values and also would reduce the property value of our homes. "But what," one member asked in a tremulous voice, "would we do if we hated a potential new neighbor." In compromise, we settled on keeping "the right of first refusal." If a potential future buyer was deemed too offensive, all the other Homeowner Association (HOA) members could buy the unit at the proffered price and then sell it to someone more to their liking.

The process of filling our complement of partners lasted about four months.[14] All during this period of partner recruitment, Green Hammer refined their cost estimates and moved toward a Guaranteed Maximum Price.

[14] Brief biographies of the eleven partners are in Appendix 1.

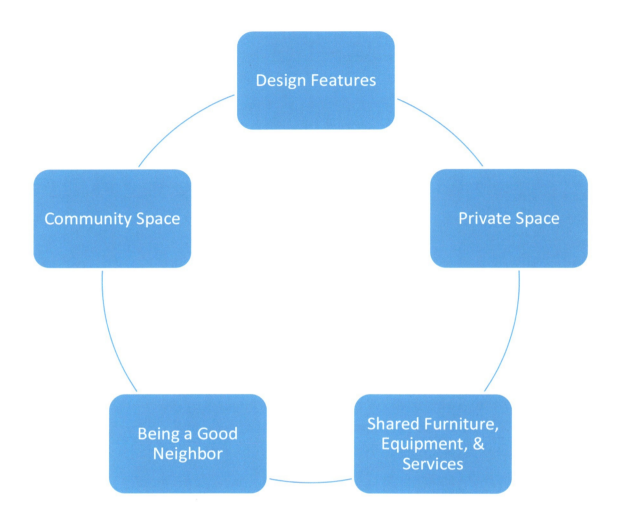

Intentional Community

As our thinking began to coalesce around the concept of living in an intentional community, we became aware of the rich history of this idea from 18th century utopias to the present. An intentional community[15] overlaps with the concept of co-housing[16] and relates to a broader concept of a sharing economy.[17]

Certain design features are necessary to create an appropriate mix between privacy and community for an intentional community; to ensure maximum use of communal space; to enhance maximum sharing of furniture, equipment, and services; and to give meaning to what "being a neighbor" means.

The back three units face the courtyard, and the second-story condo also enters from the side of the courtyard. Although the technical entrance of the two front units is on the street side, the most-used door is the back one to the courtyard. "We picked a front unit because we wanted our own entrance, but the courtyard has become so central to our group life," commented partner Roger Chope. With all houses functionally facing inward toward the courtyard, partners meet coming and going as well as nodding at guests of the others.

Although the exterior of all the units is the same and the interior space largely the same (the front two units are slightly squarer and the back three units more rectangular), their position satisfies different preferences. The front units have slightly more light and the back units have a more tucked-in feel. Each couple remains convinced they have the best location.

The five homes contain about 1,450 square feet of internal space on two floors; the first floor has an internal footprint of about 900 square feet, consisting of a master bedroom/bathroom with washer/dryer, guest bathroom, and great room (entrance, living room, dining room and kitchen). The second floor has two bedroom/offices, a landing with a library and a full bathroom.

---

[15] An "intentional community" is a group of people who have chosen to live together with a common purpose, working cooperatively to create a lifestyle that reflects their shared core values. https://cash.me/account/activity

[16] "Cohousing is an intentional community of private homes clustered around shared space. Each attached or single family home has traditional amenities, including a private kitchen. Shared spaces typically feature a common house, which may include a large kitchen and dining area, laundry, and recreational spaces. Shared outdoor space may include parking, walkways, open space, and gardens. Neighbors also share resources like tools and lawnmowers." http://www.cohousing.org/what_is_cohousing

[17] "Sharing economy is a hybrid market model (in between owning and gift giving) which refers to peer-to-peer-based sharing of access to goods and services." https://en.wikipedia.org/wiki/Sharing_economy

In addition each home has about 200 square feet of open porch on the second floor (one large south facing porch for the three back units; and a small south and larger north porch for the front units).

Common Space

The importance of the courtyard surprised us. "There is always something going on to get informal interactions started," Lainie noted. We had forsaken parking in order to dedicate a third of our land to the internal courtyard, but, in some ways, we thought that the sizeable common room would be the center of communal activities, not the courtyard. The common room is the center of much activity, but the courtyard is the heart of the community.

Dinner on Patio

In the spring, summer and fall there is common gardening of flowers, berries, trees and a vegetable garden producing an abundance of green beans, squashes, tomatoes, lettuce, and kale. From April to October, we hold community potlucks and dinners under our umbrella on the paved portion of the courtyard; but all year, we meet each other as we leave, pick up the mail, and wave at each other in the morning. "A relative said she could never live in co-housing," partner Anne Morrow confessed, "because she likes to sit outside in her bathrobe in the morning with a cup of coffee. 'Michael, in the home next to us, does that all the time,' I told her."

The common room is the most important of the shared spaces outside of the courtyard and garden. Our concept was a shared living, dining, and entertainment room more than an event space. As a result, partners will gather on the occasional evening to watch Downton Abbey or the Presidential election debates. For most of us, the common room screen is the only TV we have. At our homes, we rely on CDs or streaming. The common room also has a shared kitchen and bathroom. Generally, our individual dining rooms can seat no more than six guests comfortably. For larger events, dinners or family reunions, we reserve the common room, which with fold-up tables can serve 25. We also host meetings in the common room for social and political organizations in which partners are involved.

During our first year, one of the highlights was a dinner for all the partners in the common room featuring a meal menu from that wonderful film about a struggling new Italian restaurant, "Big Night." With fifteen people, numerous courses including a Timpano, a majestic savory pie about a foot high and foot wide, plentiful good wine, and five hours of eating and conversation, we enjoyed a great evening.

Eight of us hired a yoga instructor and hold regular Friday morning yoga in the common room at 7:30 am and on Tuesday with instructional tapes. Others attend regular Spanish classes.

Additional shared spaces include a bike room, general storage space of about 50 square feet per household, carport with a pull-up space for one car for deliveries and grocery shopping. Mailboxes are located outside the common room, and householders meet there to gossip as they collect mail. All recycling, garbage, and composting is contained in a joint shed, along with garden tools and outdoor equipment. By the nature of the community and condo association rules, all exterior maintenance of the homes is a responsibility of Ankeny Row Condominium Owners Association (ARCOA) and is handled communally.

Sharing, in general, results in less expense and time commitment because of economies of scale and avoidance of redundancy.

Private Space

The design included significant private space in each home, three bedrooms (or offices), two and half bathrooms, a great room (living/dining/kitchen), second-story porches, and a patio facing the courtyard. It is easy to find company and to be alone. There is an unspoken tradition that our communal activity takes part in shared spaces and no one is knocking on the door of other resident's homes to come in for coffee or a chat unless there is a specific reason. "I've done planning for 40 years, and there's density done right and done wrong" Dave mused. "Sitting on the bus looking into space is one sort of privacy. I love my patio and I'm out there all the time. I think we all try to sense when social interaction is good or not."

The second story porches allow partners to have their own private garden in wooden beds or pots and each home has at least two outdoor areas for eating or recreation: the deck with a table for six and first floor patio off the courtyard with a table for four. If you want to find indoor space to read or listen to music, there are choices of a window seat in one of the offices, a couch and overstuffed chair in another office or the living room. Finally, the passive house construction creates an internal environment compatible with privacy. When the triple pane windows are closed, you rarely hear external noise.

Shared Furniture, Equipment, Tools & Services

Individual homes lead to unnecessary duplication of furniture, equipment, tools and services as well as space. The community shares a barbecue grill housed in the recycling shed as well as the table and umbrella in the courtyard, our location for happy hour and potlucks during the warm months. Other shared items include ladders, garden tools, bike repair tools, books, missing ingredients for cooking and the community's one hard copy of the New York Times. In our second year, we opened a Little Free Library (LFL) and are pleased not only to have a handy way to recycle books but also note that many neighbors in a three block-radius use the LFL to both borrow and leave books and magazines.

For a single family house, maintenance and operation time is required. With a condo, organized as a sharing community, there are community meetings, unnecessary in individual homes; but many services can be done as efficiently for six families as for one, and if meetings go onto long, members have only themselves to blame. The HOA, not individual owners, takes care of home cleaning service, interior and exterior window washing, yoga, gardening, recycling, water, garbage, TV service, compost pick-up and external maintenance, such as staining outside desks.

In our early discussion of aging in place, we had thought of maintaining the smallest of the six units for rent and, if needed, a caregiver. Spreading the cost of the unit to the remaining five units would have raised the price of units by $80,000 and was unnecessary because often one or more families travel, and we use each other's homes for overflow family or friends. In addition, each of the five larger units has three bedrooms, one of which could accommodate a caregiver on the second floor.

Being a Neighbor

We look out for each other's homes. If a stranger arrives, we ask if we can "help them" to ensure they get to the right house or signal that neighbors are watching. If someone is sick or injured, other families have helped lessen the strain of shopping and other necessary daily tasks. A cohesive neighborhood is important for safety

In addition, an intentional community enhances the potential for sharing inherent in being a good neighbor: collecting the mail and FedEx packages, watering indoor plants, providing rides to the airport, swapping dog walking duties, joint carpooling to events, combined shopping runs, sharing email news of literary, artistic and political events, down to the littlest act of borrowing sugar when you run out. Of course, one can be a good neighbor in a suburban subdivision or in a community of single family homes; but it is easier in a situation where a community is consciously built. Being a good neighbor means more spontaneous contact, social interaction, and mutual assistance.

CHAPTER 5: Paying for Paradise

To bring new people into our partnership, we needed to massage the project into shape so that interested parties could evaluate it. The issues of land ownership, whether to have a developer or not, structure of the legal entity to own the project until completion and how to finance construction became paramount for us to resolve. As Green Hammer continued to refine their budgeting by obtaining subcontractor bids for our schematic design, we started outreach to find four more partners. At the outset, we decided that self-promotion and word-of-mouth would be our desired method of finding partners compatible with the project's vision and the initial two couples. See Chapter 4.

Land Title

Land ownership was initially in the name of Dick and Lavinia and Michael and Francie as tenants in common and had to be transferred to a new legal entity, Ankeny Row LLC, in order to bring in new partners. We retained a lawyer specializing in condo development and the new Ankeny Row LLC was registered with the State of Oregon. After a fascinating period of document review, an Operating Agreement and Bylaws for the LLC were formalized.[18]

As new partners commited to purchase a unit, they would invest in the land and expenses to date and become full members of the LLC. The LLC would dissolve at the time of occupancy to be replaced by condo agreements.

---

[18] The Operating Agreement and Bylaws of Ankeny Row LLC may be reviewed on https://ankenyrow.wordpress.com/

Our new lawyer also advised us to specify a project leader. In January, 2013, Lavinia was the unanimous choice as Operating Manager; Francie was chosen co-leader.

Developer Issue

We had to determine how to sell interests in the project. Our lawyer advised that the Oregon Construction Contractors Board would require a developer's license if not all the owners of Ankeny Row LLC were building units to inhabit themselves or intended to sell to others.

We had decided early on to function as "citizen developers." We would act for ourselves without a developer and no developer fee would be added to the cost of the units. Any suggestion that we would need a "developer" was anathema. However, when we added Stephen Aiguier, president of Green Hammer, as the sixth home owner to buy into the LLC for the loft condo, this problem was solved. He could obtain a developer endorsement to his general contractor license and that would take care of us in any situation. As it happened, all partners kept their units until completion of construction, converting their share of the LLC into fee simple ownership of their condo and no such endorsement was needed

Winning Stephen over as our sixth partner (See Chapter 4) also eased the insurance issue for the LLC. As contractor, Green Hammer had liability insurance and other construction insurance. Instead of the LLC having to obtain and pay for its own insurance, the LLC got coverage by an extention of the Green Hammer policy.

Financing

Green Hammer reminded Francie, Michael, Lavinia, and Dick how difficult it would be to find an appraiser to value passive house and net zero features of the project, or the courtyard, or common room. He encouraged us to pursue financing at Umpqua Bank, Green Mortgage NW, our credit unions or ShoreBank Pacific. A lender in Seattle said "maybe", but cooled later when told we intended to be our own developers in order to avoid costs, construction defect liability and licensing hurdles; and instead all partners would own the land. Eventually all but one lender said: "No" to financing our concept.

Umpqua Bank was excited about the development and pursued the problems presented by the unique approach but said appraisals would be difficult. Dick and Lavinia searched for comparables within passive house circles. Umpqua said it would not lend if the project used the tenants-in-common model. A loan officer at Washington Federal summarized obstacles we faced with the banks:

Financing Options

- Construction Loan: from bank to the developer or owners.
- Take-out mortgages: bank mortgage at the end of construction based on built unit value.
- Self financing: though home equity loan on current house.

---

1. they didn't want to finance condos in the market glut;
2. they preferred financing existing buildings to new construction;
3. they had had problems with common wall construction; and
4. condo developers were subject to a ten-year potential liability for construction defects.

Apparently 2010 was an excellent year to buy property because of declining land values in the face of the Great Recession, but 2012 was a poor time to obtain a loan, particularly for a project seen as unique.

The four partners weighed the information from lenders. The banks seemed determined to keep their money unless they could dictate the form of partner organization, charge significant loan origination fees, provide only a portion of the funding needed to build the project, and charge close to seven percent on the loan. Michael suggested partners could self-finance at lower cost with home equity loans on their existing homes.[19] Dick worried that some good prospects might not be able to self-finance, especially on relatively short notice. All agreed, however, that self-finance was appealing and solved many problems facing the project, including Green Hammer's concern about a time lag between the start of construction and the release of funds from a bank to pay subcontractors.

The last nail in the construction loan coffin came from Pacific Continental: No loan would be offered. We could have followed alternatives, such as making the LLC a developer or attempting to meet the onerous requirements of the banks; but the consensus of all four partners was that it would be better, quicker, and cheaper to self-finance.

As it happened all the partners who joined us lived in bigger and more expensive houses (after all we all were "downsizing"). All partners financed their shares of project cash calls with the proceeds from sale of their home or home equity lines of credit until eventual sale. Also, we confirmed that a number of banks would be interested in "take-out" mortgages based on the value of the newly constructed homes, if any of us wanted to take out a mortgage at the end of construction.

During this period, COLAB, an architecture firm, began developing two parcels of land immediately to the west of our property, completing construction of four buildings with a total of eight live-work spaces a year before Ankeny Row was finished. This development enhanced the attractiveness of our site and eased some concern about self-financing.

Value Engineering I

There was a budget show down in October, 2011. Green Hammer walked us through their revised construction cost estimate with bad news: the project was over our $2.25 million budget by $500,000. A series of meetings took us into "value engineering," their euphemism for cutting flesh and bone.

---

[19] Bank loan costs were 7% and up; and home equity loans were in the range of 3-4 %, a clear advantage.

Among ideas were to delay installation of photovoltaic (PV) panels; lease panels from a power company; build to code rather than passive house (PH) standards; provide options for less expensive finishes; cut square feet from the buildings. We quickly dispatched abandonment of PH and delay of installation or leasing of PV panels. We refused to move off our energy efficiency goals and hoped we would find buyers who shared our values; but we did drop square footage from the second floors and eliminated separate showers from second floor baths.

In addition, we reduced the number and sizes of some windows, narrowed the entry from Ankeny Street from 19 to 13 feet and eliminated the seating area. The smaller entry seemed more inviting and intimate. Value engineering had its positive side.

By the end of 2012 all six units were committed and in February, 2013, all partner contributions had been equalized, the property was in the ownership of Ankeny Row LLC, and Green Hammer and the owners were ready to proceed to design development.

In April, we hired Jessy Olson to monitor the construction as an Owner's Representative. She noted that any lending institution would have required such an arrangement to protect its investment. She saw things we missed, and Green Hammer was pleased with the new relationship.

Later that spring, Green Hammer reported the design phase had gone $50,000 over budget. The city had required a re-design for the flow-through planters and the common room and a higher level of design was needed on finishes and fixtures. Green Hammer offered to cover half the overrun and asked us to cover the rest. They eased the news by telling us customizations were coming in $18,000 lower than estimated. After handwringing, we agreed.

Green Hammer filed applications for permits in the third week of June with a full set of construction drawings and now sought bids from over 100 purveyors of labor and materials from nails to PV panels. This would allow Green Hammer to finally remove "allowances" (items with no guaranteed price) in the draft Schedule of Values (SOV), their name for a budget, and tell partners what their units would really cost. They issued a new warning that material and labor costs were rising with a recovering housing market and that they were having trouble getting the attention of producers and subcontractors to make bids.

Value Engineering II

A new SOV came in early August, 2013, based upon the bids: the project would cost $350,000 more than the early 2012 estimate, a 15 percent increase. Partner gasps were audible. ZOLA windows and doors were up 25 percent. The Parr Lumber bid for base cabinetry rose 30 percent. Geopiers would cost $9,000 more than the $50,000 estimate. Even PV panels had risen and incentives had dropped. Revisions to the plans required by the city—especially the flow-through planters—were costing design time and extra materials and labor.

Jessy helped the bad news go down. "To put the design costs in perspective, you've come in with design costs at around 12.5% of the total hard costs. This is above average -- typically I would expect a project of this size to come in the 9-10% range -- but you have a final product that the team has put a lot of thought and care into, that is above and beyond the typical 'sustainable home' model, that is customized for you and your long-term plans."

We now faced "Value Engineering, Part II." Our target was to cut the overrun by half. GH recommended fewer PV panels, 12 per unit rather than 13. Further modeling showed 12 panels might get us to net zero. If not, there was room above to add panels later. This got thumbs up as did a plan that reduced hardscaping costs by substituting boulders in place of pre-fab walls in the courtyard and pavers in place of concrete on most of the terrace. The new materials and more sinuous pathways made the courtyard and terrace seem less formal, less French, more country English. After much discussion, we eliminated the sauna. We postponed the hot tub; we would plumb for it and decide whether to install it after move-in. We delayed installation of the glass pergola over a portion of the courtyard terrace and the entry portal. We decided to wait until after construction and see how satisfied we were without them.

Changes to exterior siding presented the largest savings. Partners switched from stucco to HardiePanel on first floors and from the original HardiePanel on second floors to less expensive 4" HardiePlank lap siding, a significant saving. Eventually even the stucco lovers thought the Hardie panels looked better.

We rejected elimination of the second floor decks. We also saved the distinctive metal railings around the decks (GH had offered cedar) for design distinction and lower maintenance costs. No reduction in the number or size of windows; light was too precious. No substitution of Simpson front doors for the amazing Zolas ($2,800 each); that would cost Ankeny Row PH certification. No also to reducing the size of the common room kitchen.

Green Hammer had proposed substitution of asphalt shingles for metal roofing, a savings of $30,000. This generated more buzz than elimination of the sauna. Durability, maintenance and aesthetics weighed against the savings. Metal roofs last 45-60 years, asphalt roofing 35. Partners preferred the look of metal. But some argued the roofing material would not be visible from the street. Those who would live in the back countered that asphalt on Building A *would* be visible to them. Desperate for savings, we tentatively went for asphalt, on a rare split vote.

To sweeten the savings total, Green Hammer said they would reduce costs by one percent ($15,000), to be achieved through tougher negotiations with subs. With this, the total savings reached $153,000, and accounting for higher material costs and the value engineering we had done to date and an estimate of the customization we intended to do for each unit, the cost for each of the five condos had risen to $630,000.

Weeks later, we returned to our roof decision. Several thought a metal roof was aesthetically superior to asphalt. Green Hammer noted other advantages: PV panels clip onto a metal roof, making installation and later addition of panels easier, and there would no need for a support structure with nails penetrating the asphalt shingles. That did it; back to metal roofs. The change of mind proved one of our happiest.

Then on September 24, 2013, we held our official groundbreaking, even though it preceded the actual beginning of construction by two months.

Groundbreaking

Partners had expected to sign a construction contract – "Design Build Institute of America #535" (DBIA)–with a Guaranteed Maximum Price (GMP), prior to construction. We understood the DBIA would have a Schedule of Values (SOV) with allowances. But Green Hammer was having difficulty getting solid bids from subs in many areas, due in part to the rising construction market. The seemingly never-ending customization process was also a culprit. Mild recriminations flowed over the delay. Green Hammer thought individual partner decision-making took too long on customizations and upgrades. Partners attributed some of the delay to Green Hammer's risk aversion, some to the inability of GH to provide timely "base" cost information in relation to "upgrade" and "customization" costs.

Intent on moving ahead, we agreed to start the next phase of construction with a Limited Notice to Proceed (LNP)[20]. Months passed with a string of revisions to the LNP; instead of a GMP contract, we had a time-and-materials contract. On advice from Jessy, we informed Green Hammer we would sign no further revisions to the LNP. Green Hammer would have to remove the allowances and accept the risk of cost increases to be deducted from its four percent contingency

Green Hammer sent the proposed "final" SOV to us on December 17, 2013. Costs were $28,000 higher than shown in the August SOV, attributable to the underground storage tanks and a trolley line encountered under Ankeny Street, which needed removal; a mistake in price for interior paint; an error in calculation of the size of footings to guard against frost; brackets that needed rafter tailings on the back units; better bike racks following research; and special tape for the Polish windows omitted from a bill.

Both sides were determined to come to terms on a final DBIA before Christmas. Stephen found another way to cut costs: reduce the number of PV panels serving the common room to six. That saved $15,000. Jessy focused on the cost increases from the August SOV. She argued Green Hammer would have had to draw on the four percent contingency to cover these increases had the GMP been in place. Instead, the risk fell entirely on the LLC. She suggested Green Hammer go halfway on the increase; they resisted with their eye on the bottom line.

Jessy turned to the remaining allowances, challenging Green Hammer's approach of carrying allowances until precise costs are nailed down, accepting no risk while holding on to four percent contingency. Stephen agreed to remove allowances for appliances, the east fence, wiring and the mailboxes. We agreed to extend the remaining big allowance for cabinets, but put a deadline on settling it. Stephen sweetened the pot by offering to install cork floor in the common room at cost.

We were not finished with DBIA negotiations when the time to advance a retainer of 15 percent of the total contract price to ensure Green Hammer could make timely payment of

---

[20] A LNP is **not** a guaranteed price contract but rather essentially an agreement that we, the owners, would pay labor costs at an agreed hourly rate and materials and outside consultants at cost plus 20% markup.

subcontractors and advance purchase of materials (approximately $335,000) arrived. There was no indication that Green Hammer was in trouble, but we had agreed to a non-standard contract provision for such a retainer. What if they went bankrupt during construction of our project, their biggest to date? What chance would we have to recover any of the retainer? Retired lawyers think about these things. There was another concern: according to Jessy it is not uncommon for builders to divert retainers from one project to cover immediate expenses on another.

Our solution was to offer to place the retainer in escrow. Green Hammer would show how a draw would be spent and would need LLC approval before drawing from the retainer; but they balked at this solution. A shuffle of phone calls led to a compromise. Green Hammer would cut their retainer in half to reduce our risk of loss if we agreed to a contract adjustment. If they acquired materials at a lower cost than specified in the SOV, Green Hammer would keep any savings as it had become clear their profit margin was shrinking. Previously the agreement was that Green Hammer and the LLC would split such savings.

On December 23, 2013, the Ankeny Row LLC signed a contract with Green Hammer with a guaranteed maximum price, which took us through construction. At this same time, the partners became aware of escalating "off contract" expenses: street closure permits; attorney fees for HOA documents; the reserves study and landscaping, which would drive up unit costs somewhat. Landscaping presented a peculiar set of issues. There was $35,000 in the SOV for landscaping, but that was insufficient for everything we wanted. Should we do the planting ourselves to save money? Should we add the uncovered items to the SOV? Or, should we keep these separate, hire our own sub, thereby exempting the costs from the contract mark-up?

Spirits which had been lifted by groundbreaking receded quickly as fall rains began. Three months after application, the city had not issued permits. We bickered with Green Hammer over the precision in reporting necessary to allow partners to track costs. They had billed construction manager hours to the design stage. Lavinia raised a July promise that construction management hours would be billed to the construction phase to begin after groundbreaking and the new contract with a guaranteed maximum price (GMP) had been signed. She persuaded Green Hammer to bill the time as promised.

Finally, in January 2014, the framing began to rise. Constuction had begun and it now would be full speed ahead.

Framing

We spent detailed time on this pre-construction phase of developing a budget, value engineering and financing not because we had an especially rough time. Actually, the opposite. We had no overwhelming challenges and dealt with glitches as they came up. Our relationship with Green Hammer was almost uniformly great. We trusted them, loved their design and craftsmanship and enjoyed them as individuals. If we were able to represent their viewpoint adequately, they would certainly have many valid criticisms of our developer group of eleven strong-willed individuals.

However, we want to draw some general lessons from our experience:

- It is possible to come in under budget, but, in general, with individuals who are considering where they will live, **costs are going to go up** as they have to decide between cheaper option A and more desirable option B. If your group will implode with rising costs, a construction project is not for you.
- **Budgets and bids come first; construction comes later.** In our case, two years later. Costs can go down for materials, subcontractors, etc, but they do not generally do so.

- **An Owner's Representative**, such as Jessy Olson, is vital. One needs someone knowledgeable, who can interface with the contractors and argue points of contract, cost, or building logic, where necessary.
- To pull off a project like Ankeny Row requires **flexibility** in regard to financing, costs, contract provisions, and maybe most important being able to see not only your own point of view but also that of others such as your contractor, who are responding to different pressures.

Chapter 6: Documents, Documents

We knew there would be documents. We'd bought and sold many homes over the decades. Each transaction generated a blizzard of documents and carpal tunnel pains from signing disclosures. Documents for Ankeny Row would be more voluminous, of course. We just didn't know there would be *that* many, they would be *so* long, or *so* blooming boiler-plated and convoluted. But it was good we didn't fully comprehend the scale and scope of the documents. We believed the three lawyers among the two founding couples could do it ourselves, undaunted by the facts that we were retired and none of us had been a real estate lawyer. To save money and self-respect, we started drafting.

We had put title to the land in the names of the two couples, anticipating we would establish a limited liability corporation (LLC) once the heat of the transaction dissipated. The partners in our stillborn Tillamook enterprise had created an LLC, which would be our model for Ankeny Row. Our plan was to transfer title from the two couples to the new LLC. Then, when we were ready, we would add partners to the LLC.

"Ready" meant we had a design and a budget to show prospective partners. We wanted a design for the project before taking on a fully battery of partners because we were in a hurry. We'd "lost" several years from the failed Tillamook effort and we knew involving as many as 12 to 14 people early in the design process would bog us down. We also thought most people don't want to devote hours and hours to decision-making, particularly if they have no certainty anything would come of it. They'd prefer to see a design that had some momentum behind it and a detailed budget showing a cost they could afford. Four of us could get us there much faster. A "Schematic Design"[21] would give us detailed drawings and renderings and a detailed, reliable estimate of the cost of a unit.

For the LLC we needed the establishment document to file with the state, an Operating Agreement and Bylaws.[22] Besides looking to our Tillamook documents (we fondly called them "docs"), we went to the web for models. Good fortune took us to Eli Spevak of Orange Splot, developer of several co-housing projects. Public-spirited and generous with his expertise and time, he sent us to the website of Cully Grove, his latest co-housing project. An advocate for co-housing and other unconventional housing types and community living, he invited us to plagiarize the Cully Grove LLC documents, which we did, shamelessly.

Eli focused us on a basic question: what would be the form of ownership? Condos? A "planned unit development" (PUD) with a platted lot for each residence and common areas owned by some other entity? He laid out pros and cons. Subdivisions are easier for phasing development and infrastructure can be less expensive. Condos involve a lot of docs and, he warned, lots of attorney fees. A PUD would require city approval of a subdivision, a process that could take six months or more and involves significant fees. Impatience and unwarranted confidence in our drafting skills tilted us toward the condo model. Sensing our DIY penchant, Eli gently suggested we pursue the ownership question with a real estate lawyer. Since he is himself is a DIY person, we valued his advice and visited his lawyer.

She spotted "the issue" immediately. Our plan called for a common room with a condo above it. PUD regulations, she said, would not accommodate this unconventional division of ownership. That settled it: we would do condos.

Then she threw a potential roadblock in our DIY path: to act as our own developer we would need to be licensed as a "developer" in order to sell units. This was not what we wanted to hear. We wanted to be "citizen developers" and we wanted to avoid developer fees. We took this

---

[21] Schematic Design is an initial design scheme that seeks to define the general scope and conceptual design of the project including scale and relationships between building components. At the end of the schematic design phase the architect/designer will present some very rough sketches to the owners for approval.

[22] Ankeny Row LLC Operating Agreement and Bylaws may be found at https://ankenyrow.wordpress.com/

problem home to mull, but solved this problem when the president of Green Hammer signed on for the sixth unit.

The lawyer-partners got busy. First, we wrote the basic LLC doc to register with the state. Then we waded into the operating agreement and the bylaws. With only four talking heads, we got to agreement on contents with little friction. With drafts ready, we DIY lawyers came to our senses and sent the docs to the lawyer for "quick review." It wasn't quick, but it was good. After back and forth that tried our patience, she filed the docs with the state and the LLC was launched. Still more docs — a contract to transfer ownership of the property from the two couples to Ankeny Row LLC; a new deed making the LLC the owner of the property; and a limited Power of Attorney so Lavinia could sign for Francie and Michael while they were out of the country — flooded our files.

The docs provided that prospective partners could reserve a unit for a refundable deposit (for which our lawyer composed a "receipt" of a length out of proportion to the amount of the deposit). Anyone waiting to commit risked being upstaged by someone with a quicker trigger finger. When ready, prospects would invest in the land and design expenses to date and become full partners. When all units were committed, we would amend the LLC documents (the "First Amended Operating Agreement") to reflect the new owners. At project completion, the LLC would dissolve and be replaced by a condominium owners association.

After all partners had made their investments and become full partners in Ankeny Row, the lawyer-partners got busy on the docs that would replace the LLC docs: Declaration, Operating Agreement and Bylaws. These were the docs to set up Ankeny Row Condominium Owners Association (ARCOA) and establish the rules of operation. We had the drafting drill down. We adapted models we found at condo websites and sent them to the real estate lawyer for review. We then introduced the drafts to partners for discussion.[23]

The discussion was revelatory for the partners. We'd already had 18 months of "seasoning" in the "design development" process. We'd made scores of easy and difficult decisions on

---

[23] Samples of a Declaration, Bylaws and Operating Agreement for ARCOA are available at https://ankenyrow.wordpress.com/

project design (hot tub in the courtyard?) and cutting costs (substitute asphalt for metal roofs?) and were confident we could handle anything that came our way. But Homeowners Association (HOA) issues are different, some personal, some ideological, even the nerdy issues can raise hackles. There were some unspoken anxieties.

Lawyer-partners guided other partners through the docs, warming up with dry governance matters. Composition of the HOA board? Egalitarian and participatory instincts had led us to think we should all sit on the HOA board. The lawyer recommended a small board to make decision-making easier. She noted most HOA business is tedious. Achieving quorums would be especially difficult among retired people who love to travel. Lawyer-partners reminded others that all partners elect the board, can remove board members, can repeal or revise rules adopted by the board and control the coveted reserve fund. We settled on a three-person board.

Allocation of expenses perked everybody up. First, who owns what? It seemed straightforward. Ankeny Row would be a condominium. After all, each partner owns the inside of the unit; the ARCOA (with each household in ARCOA owning a pro rata share of common areas) owns the outside of each unit and all the common facilities, such as the common room. It is not straightforward.

Our Declaration establishes three types of ownership: individual units, common areas and limited common areas. We put the line between unit and common area at the studs, including the unexposed surface of the sheetrock nailed to the studs. Outside surfaces of windows and doors are common, inside surfaces belong to the unit.[24] The Declaration does run on about floors, ceilings and ducts. We gave special attention to photovoltaic panels – on the roof and common elements–to ensure each owner could take advantage of federal and state tax credits and deductions (not available to HOAs).

Patios, decks and some courtyard paths fall into the limited common area category. Rights and responsibilities are mixed between owners and ARCOA in these areas. We wrote provisions to sort that out. Owners can put planters on their decks, for example, without approval of the

---

[24] The HOA board advised each unit owner to obtain coverage from the same company hired by the board to cover common areas to make it easier to settle insurance claims.

HOA. The HOA is responsible for the rest of the common areas, such as the courtyard and common room.

Once everybody understood who owns what (or thought they did), it became easier to grasp the allocation of expenses. Our Declaration provided that costs of upkeep and repair of common elements would be shared equally, not by investment shares. Capital expenses in common areas, on the other hand, would be allocated among owners by the investment shares set at the time partners became members of the LLC (based principally on the size of units).

Now warmed up, we turned to more engaging issues. What about dogs in the courtyard? "OK on a leash." They could be leashless in the common room, where good behavior was expected. Smoking? Of course not! Not anywhere!...except the weed we inhaled in college (later legalized in Oregon). "Make the bylaws say no *tobacco*!" Political signs? "OK inside units; none in the courtyard." What about politically incorrect signs? Victory for the First Amendment! We could display anything from socialist slogans to posters of the Dead. Can owners rent their units? "Yes, but not for terms shorter than 30 days." House exchanges? "OK." Decision-making was so smooth and agreeable we began to worry about ourselves. It wasn't the weed; none of us had any.

Did following the DIY path make us feel better about ourselves or save us money? We probably did save a bit of money by spending hours drafting and discussing documents but recognized when to step off the path and run to the real estate lawyer. Most importantly though, we actually understood the docs by the time we filed them.

On March 9, 2016, a year after new owners moved into their units, partners in the LLC passed the torch to their new selves, unit-owners and members of ARCOA. Our long-suffering and perseverant operating manager Lavinia performed her last task months later: filing the documents to terminate Ankeny Row LLC.

CHAPTER 7: Design-Build in Action

Design began in earnest once all partners invested in the LLC. The initial partners had taken things through "Schematic Design,"[25] far enough for floor plans, renderings of the building elevations and a detailed estimate of costs, but not enough, of course, to guide actual construction. Now it was time for "Design Development,"[26] the basis for construction drawings. All of us would be at the design table with the Green Hammer team.

We were confident that the design-build model would yield the benefits for which it is touted: better, more practical design from close, constant communication between in-house architects and in-house builders; savings of time and money from close coordination between the designers and the builders.

Inexperience reared its ugly head, right at the beginning of design development. Green Hammer and the initial partners had invested a lot of time and money in the schematic design. Was it the Sacred Stone? Between the founding partners and Green Hammer there was an unspoken (unfortunately) notion that the fundamentals of the design were, if not sacred, at least beatified. Partners would, of course, choose wall colors, tile grouts and appliances. But change the floor plan to eliminate the powder bath for a wine cellar? Sacrilege!

Green Hammer and the initial partners could have taken a firm stand. Instead, in our ardor to move forward and get commitments, we hedged. More importantly, we came to understand

---

[25] See footnote 21.

[26] Design development is the phase in which all important aspects of the project are defined and described so that all that remains is the formal documentation step of construction contract documents, materials and building systems.

that these dwellings would likely be our last before the institution. We'd always bought "used" houses designed by someone else. This was our chance to design exactly what we wanted.

For better or worse, we drifted into the complex world of tracking changes in design and their costs; it tested the design-build model mightily. It was better because the 'newbies" who hadn't participated in schematic design now put their fingerprints on their units and the whole project. Each set of partners made the design of their unit their own. But we paid a price in time, frustration and money.

Partner's Design Meeting

Green Hammer gave us a system with a built-in disincentive for significant changes. The schematic design and its accompanying budget ("Schedule of Values," or SOV) served as the "base." The lowest order changes were "upgrades." If the SOV allowed $1,000 for the fridge and a partner wanted a super-efficient Liebherr, the partner would pay the difference in cost. Next were the "customizations." If a partner wanted two sinks in the master bath instead of the one in the design, the partner would pay not only for the second sink, but a 10 percent markup for re-design of the counter. The most grievous deviation was a "change order." If a partner wanted to change the floor plan to move a wall to add storage, the partner would pay for the cost of the change from the design and a 20 percent markup.

This system worked when Green Hammer had established the "base" for an item, such as a dishwasher; but it soon became apparent that determining the cost difference between "base" and most finishes, fixtures and furnishings was elusive, in part because they had trouble parsing out the base cost. Given the number of items and variety of models, pricing all the options became an enormous undertaking. Partners found it difficult to make a responsible choice until presented the cost of each "base" item. Six custom homes and a common room stretched Green Hammer's accounting systems to the breaking point. They responded by revising their cost accounting and devoting more time to tracking. Nonetheless, tracking the choices and determining the cost delta would vex the design process to the last tile grout choice. Trust and a sense of common endeavor shared by Green Hammer and partners sustained us through this trying period.

The schematic design showed three buildings arrayed around a courtyard. Building A fronted Ankeny Street and contained two attached townhouses. Building B was composed of three attached townhouses on the back side of the site facing the courtyard. Building C faced Ankeny Street, and the ground floor would house the common room, bike storage and storage cages for each condo. The second floor was an apartment. The townhouses would have about 1,450 square feet of internal space each and the apartment about 865 square feet. Design development did not disturb this general layout in the schematic design. Otherwise, design development became a moveable feast.

Courtyard Rendering
Drawing by Daryl Rantis, Lead Architect for Green Hammer

The first revisions were satisfying because they flowed from the design process as we'd imagined it: design-build in action. Green Hammer software displayed sunlight on the courtyard and the rear units in every season, every time of day and every roof configuration and pitch. The exercise led us to abandon the gabled roofs on Building A in the schematic design. See Chapter 2 for more discussion and design of gables.

Further mouse-play showed that sloping the roof of Building A down toward the courtyard would open things up. On the spot, the build side of Green Hammer suggested the roof of Building B should also pitch south toward the courtyard. The Building B roof had capacity for all the PV panels we would need. And the pitch south would allow small clerestory windows on the north side of B to lighten up second floors. The clerestories would also help flush heat that would rise to second floors in summer months. There would be greater heat loss through these northern windows. But modeling showed solar radiation through the expanded window schedule on the south side would compensate.

Green Hammer invited a co-housing specialist to an early design session. The discussion inspired re-orientation of the common room entrance from the entryway between Buildings A and C to the courtyard. Partners later concluded this revision was one of the design ideas that made our courtyard so conducive to chance encounters and exchanges among partners.

Events during design development forced Green Hammer and partners to make changes. This tested the design-build model: the architects and the builders batted ideas about in meetings with partners. Partners looked at options, listened to pros and cons, and decided. We gained confidence in Green Hammer and the model; and they gained confidence in partners' reasoning and readiness to decide.

Code requirements turned our garage into a carport, like it or not. We decided to like it. One result was expansion of the bike room; it would accommodate 12 rather than ten bikes. It turned out that every partner had at least one bike, making 12 spots essential to partner comity.

The code also forced changes to the common room located on the ground floor of Building C. A code person in the city's Bureau of Development Services (BDS) looked at the drawings and asked what the space was. "A common room", said the architect. Then came the surprise. "It can't be a common room under the code because it has an apartment above it." Green Hammer brought this to partners and presented the options offered by BDS: we'd have to design the common room as a commercial or a residential space. If commercial, we'd have to upgrade the kitchen and enhance the fire suppression system (sprinklers). If residential, we'd have to add a full bath, a closet and two-hour firewall between the residence/common room and the adjoining condo storage. To minimize additional cost, partners elected "residential." One partner noted we might want to convert it to a seventh residence after the apocalypse. A high note for design-build: the forced re-design of the condo storage room sparked a reorientation that reduced the number of doors and reduced cost.

The green eyeshades at BDS caught another peccadillo: Building B was too close to the north property line. We'd have to "move" it one foot south. Partners were not pleased by this announcement. Fault of design-side or build-side? We were presented two possibilities: keep the footprint and push one foot into the courtyard or shrink the footprints of the three back townhouses. The decision was easier than partners anticipated. Even before we'd hired GH we'd done research on successful courtyards. The courtyard was sacred ground.

Christopher Alexander[27] illustrated what he deemed the ideal ratio between the size of the courtyard and the bulk of buildings that surround it. We tested it in courtyards in our old neighborhoods and found that the ratio seemed right; we designed the courtyard with the ratio in mind. It was unanimous: save courtyard space, reduce the footprints. GH design-build went to work and suggested larger rooms and decks on second floors. We jumped at it. A consequence was that most partners – still climbing stairs with aplomb – put their master bedrooms on the second floor, ready to move downstairs if necessary.

Then there were the budget "events" that forced design changes. See Chapter 5, Paying for Paradise. Three times GH presented us with updated SOVs during the schematic design phase. In none of them did overall costs go down (an unnatural occurrence in the construction world). Our first sharp-penciled estimate of the cost of each townhouse was $570,000, including

[27] *A Pattern Language*

land; and this was the basis of our bottom line and Green Hammer's first construction budget. Seasoned by some years, partners anticipated costs would rise to account for inflation if nothing worse happened. Inflation happened. So did other "events." We watched our initial estimate recede like the contrails behind the flights to Seattle.

We had convened for what Green Hammer called "value engineering" (VE) three times during schematic design. VE was first and foremost a test of our values. We could bring the cost of Ankeny Row back to the original cost estimates simply by building to code rather than passive house standards and dropping PV panels. No partner wanted to do that. Instead, we made other cuts. VE was a chance for the design-build model to shine, and it often did. In the cutting room, the design side, the build side and the partners came up with solutions that were well designed, practical and brought the budget down from the stratosphere.

But the weather was cloudy sometimes in the design development and construction phase with design-build. We learned how important open lines of communication between design and build are. Good communication seemed especially challenging when the subs arrived. They were usually not in the picture when Green Hammer/partner meetings were happening. Design-build success with subs on the scene relies heavily on the communication skills of the project manager, who becomes the two-way interpreter between the sub and the design team.

Once the dust settled we asked ourselves whether the design-build model met our expectations. We had to admit our expectations were high, perhaps too high for the complexity of Ankeny Row with its customizations and change orders. Design-build short circuited mostly over little things. One sub helped an owner choose a hallway light fixture with a flat base, but the ceiling sloped in that hallway. The sub didn't know. There were a few larger misses. Another sub raised the level of the courtyard garden near the front units several inches to slow the flow of water across the courtyard from the back units. One of the front units then took on water during a rainstorm. A French drain solved the problem; but better design-build communication would have prevented the problem.

As with decisions we made about the contents of our documents (see Chapter 6, Documents, Documents), we surprised ourselves at our smooth and efficient decision-making, although some occasionally thought we'd wasted time in meetings that went on too long. Also, as another variant on aging-in-place, we wanted desperately to finish and occupy Ankeny Row while still living.

Green Hammer hurried to complete construction drawings to accompany applications for building permits to beat the start date of July 1, 2013, to avoid a significant increase in systems development charges to support off-site systems, such as sewer, water and parks. We still struggled over the terms of the construction contract with Green Hammer, but anticipation of breaking ground and pouring concrete was almost overwhelming. The design development phase drew to a close.

CHAPTER 8: The Tonka Toys Arrive

With contract negotiations dragging on about "allowances," Operating Manager Lavinia signed a "limited notice to proceed"[28] on September 18, 2013. It authorized Green Hammer to excavate the site, drive the geopiers and pour the foundations. We were ready to start construction; we just needed building permits.

Meanwhile, we learned Dr. Wolfgang Feist, Director of the PassivHaus Institut and popularizer of PH in Europe, would visit Portland on a speaking tour. It was his practice to visit a local PH project on his visits, if one was available. He chose Ankeny Row. The visit, set for September 24, would be filmed as part of a documentary on PH and his devotion to it. We decided we would break ground that day, permits or not.

The good Dr. Feist's visit beat the permits by three weeks. He turned dirt with us, witnessed by media and 50 people. PH was happening all over the world, he said. The technology was open and available to everyone. Most important, unlike many mechanical systems-based methods of reducing energy use, PH has delivered the 90 percent reduction promised.

On the last day of September, the city Bureau of Development Services (BDS) issued addresses for each unit. This, we thought, augured imminent issuance of permits. BDS told us "October 8." But it didn't happen.

A bug in permit approval popped up, having to do with the common room sprinkler system. It took two visits by project manager Patrick Kiblinger to BDS to break through the bureaucratic crust. Now the permit was to come on October 11. It didn't.

---

[28] See footnote 19 and Chapter 5.

At last, we learned we could pick up the permits upon presentation of a check for $108,000. This included permit fees ($53,000) and specified systems development charges (SDCs) ($55,000). We plunked down the formidable sum and walked out with building permits. It was October 16. Despite what felt like forever, BDS had beaten the 120-day deadline set in state law.

It was a brilliant fall, dry and clear. Then construction began. The Tonka Toys, as Dave called them, appeared on a rainy October 25 to pull the stumps of the Trees of Heaven from the north boundary. Heaven took its revenge: rain and removal of the stumps destabilized the Portland General Electric (PGE) utility pole. PGE, searching for a new location for the pole, discovered a no-build easement where they wanted to move it. Operating Manager Lavinia wondered how the easement could have escaped the Title Report. A furious search of documents and memories revealed it was the now-retired city easement for fire-fighting access to the late warehouse. Its retirement had escaped PGE.

Tonka Toys

Ankeny Row needed a dry well for the water retention system. Subcontractors dug it in the midst of fall rains. If it drained, we would need only one well; if not, we'd need two and $10,000 more. We held our collective breaths. After several days of testing, the geo-tech master said "it drains!"

Driving pilings to support foundations in the unconsolidated soils was the next big step. Starting at the end of October, three large backhoes augured holes and drove piles to 30 feet. The pounding shook buildings on all sides and rankled nerves two blocks off. A dentists' office lay directly behind us. On the second day of tremors, the dentists asked for a suspension so they could install a crown. Patrick put the tumult on pause for two hours and saved the relationship.

Two days into the pile driving, workers encountered two separate 18-inch-thick concrete slabs five feet below grade. Excavators arrived next day, broke up the slabs and removed them. OM Lavinia was relieved. "At least they didn't find an underground oil tank!"

Drilling for Pilings

Next day the pile drivers encountered an underground oil tank. It was a 2,000-gallon tank full of diesel. We were lucky: the tank hadn't leaked and excavators were already on site. After a remediation truck pumped the oil, the excavator removed the tank. OM Lavinia cheerily informed partners the cost of the extra work would be covered from savings from having to dig only one dry well.

One day later the crew hit a second, smaller oil tank. It was empty. OM Lavinia sprouted gray hair roots. Had it leaked? How much soil would have to be removed? How long would it take? Lucky again: the tank hadn't leaked. It was out of the ground before Lavinia could file her report. "Dig no more holes!" she ordered, learning quickly the limits of her power.

The next day's call reported a broken augur. Work stopped. A search turned up a replacement. The crew finished the last of 158 geo-piers on November 9. The four-day job took eight.

Pipes for utilities were "undergrounded." Grading moved along smartly, though the unconsolidated soils seemed to swallow the "structural fill" dumped by giant earth movers in great gulps. A sub placed 16-inch-thick slabs of foam insulation to 'wrap' the foundation, the first sign we were building to passive house standards. Partners felt warm just looking at the foam and the surprise benefit of added strength against earthquake was comforting, as we'd all read the article about the Big One in Kathy Schultz's article in the *New Yorker*.

Meanwhile, we had another surprise. The city sewer under Ankeny Street wasn't where city drawings indicated. The sub doing our hookup adjusted his excavation and hit an ancient trolley track from the Twenties. Everything stopped while Patrick got permission from the city to cut the track. Being transit freaks, we wanted a slice of track for display in the common room. Patrick flashed his Mona Lisa smile; that meant "not gonna happen."

The unpleasant surprises that had been coming our way– the strange concrete slab five feet below a portion of the surface; the two undetected oil tanks; unconsolidated soils that required pilings to support foundations; and flow-through planters to slow the drainage of rainwater to the storm water system and others - made their presence known to the budget. Even after a third round of "value engineering", the cost for the base unit had risen to $610,000.

Contract negotiations finally produced agreement. The construction completion date was specified as September 18, 2014 (360 days after the date the parties agreed was the date of commencing construction under the Limited Notice to Proceed). This meant the risk of increased prices for items in the seven-page SOV spreadsheet shifted from Ankeny Row LLC to Green Hammer. After getting thumbs up from partners, Lavinia signed the DBIA with a final budget, or "schedule of values" (SOV), and the coveted guaranteed maximum price (GMP) in December, 23, 2013.

On the day after Christmas, the concrete sub poured the footings and slab for Building B, home of the three rear units. It looked like a flight deck with periscopes up. Framing topped the slab on Unit 5 the day after New Year's, 2014. We took a look; the rooms appeared at once too

Slab in Wrap

small and too large. "Wait for the sheetrock; it'll seem right then," seasoned builder Patrick said.

Builders say things go thrillingly fast at the beginning and agonizingly slow at the end. By mid-January, 2014, the three back units of Building B had taken shape. Huge trucks hauled rock or cement, maneuvering carefully among dozens of pipes sticking out of the ground, guided by "drivers" standing on the ground with devices in hand.

By the end of January, subflooring for the second stories of the rear units covered the first floors. Later that week the walls of the second floor rose and the trusses of the roof over the first floor sloped toward the courtyard. Stairs appeared in each rear unit; expectant occupants were able to stride upon their second floors. By early February, sheathing topped the second floors, ready for sealing materials and insulation. The pace was breathtaking; some of us visited every day.

Framing Floor

Forms in Snow

Snow fell in February. Work froze. "Delays because of weather will come out the other end," Stephen warned the contractual completion date would extend for Force Majeure Events, i.e. bad weather. Water dripped through the sheathing onto the floors. Graffiti showed up. This was winter. But the "openings" – windows and doors from Zola in Poland - were reported steaming through the Panama Canal, the route chosen so the argon between panes wouldn't burst crossing the Continental Divide.

Foam insulation appeared at the front of the site, to surround footings and the slab for Building A (Units 1 and 2). Slabs were poured into the foam early in March. Rafters were placed for the roof of Building B in back. Things were cooking again.

Partners got to talking about the cedar elements of the exterior design: belly bands, lintels above doors, fascias, deck planking, rafter tails, beams supporting entry overhangs and the rest. Green Hammer intended to let the cedar weather for aesthetics and reduction of maintenance cost. Most partners wanted the different beauty of stained cedar. We had another chance to test our consensus-building. We succeeded: all exterior cedar would be stained rather than left bare. We

Staining Tails

no longer surprised one another; we now expected successful decision-making and got it again and again.

Because staining was not in the GMP, we offered to do it ourselves. We'd save the cost of staining and get our hands dirty on the project. The Green Hammer team was genuinely impressed, with our determination and our naiveté. They set up a staining room at their offices and showed us what to do. There were scores of 12-foot fascia boards piled on palettes. Each board needed two coats, each coat took an overnight to dry. The maturity of our years brought us to reality: months of blisters, back pain, project delay and lost opportunity with grandchildren versus the added cost of about $7,000 per partner. The partners took turns and finished the rafter tails, slowly and deliberately. Then we turned our brushes over to the professionals.

Windows and doors arrived early March, stored in high security containers on the site. The largest window weighed 800 pounds and would require a crane for installation. They were formidable and beautiful. GH installed the first Zola window, a small one in the north side of Unit 4. Installation demonstrated one aspect of PH construction: the very thick walls (just under16 inches) could support the tilt position of the very heavy windows.

Door

Door Edge

Now Ankeny Street was abuzz with the movement of machines and workers, to the "delight" of the dentists and neighbors on the street. The second small apartment project of our neighbor CoLab to the west began sinking pilings in March. Two larger apartment projects added to the din. One lane was closed to cyclists and motorists alike, indefinitely. We heard about it from frustrated cyclists. "We're cyclists, too!" we offered. Promises it would be over in September (later proved wrong) brought a fragile peace.

Dark bronze metal roof sections lowered onto Building C in early April, 2014. The bronze complemented the stained Maranti wood frames of the Zola windows and doors. In stark contrast, the blue wrap and the extraordinary white Swiss-made Siga sealing tape promised a tight envelope and presented a striking tableau.

Building A shot up with the April flowers. By the end of the month Green Hammer was erecting first and second-floor trusses. Buildings A and B were now at full height; it was possible to get a feeling for the space of the courtyard. Instincts that the hot tub would intrude too massively into the courtyard were validated; we'd made the right decision to drop it.

Trusses

Trusses Installed

May concentrated on Building C (common room with condo above), which came last because its foundation would cut off access by trucks and lifts to the courtyard and the rear units. Nevertheless, the electrician remained busy wiring back units. One consequence was the need to slap plywood over door and window openings to prevent copper wire theft.

The second half of May saw major progress on Building A. Framing the exterior was completed. Preparations were made for the roofs and exterior sheathing. Heat recovery ventilators (HRVs) were installed. Units 3, 4 and 5 in Building B were fully wired and ready for electrical inspection and sheetrock. Owners were seen pacing off the lengths of their dining rooms to see if their tables would fit.

We knew it was coming. In the third week of May, Green Hammer reported that a combination of a short-handed construction crew, sick days and weather stalls would delay occupancy to November 1. We'd lost a month. The DBIA imposed a penalty for late completion. Lawyer-partners reread the contract and were surprised to be reminded that the penalty did not kick in until 90 days after the contract completion date. That would take us to December 18. Stephen comforted his clients by saying Green Hammer costs for delay far exceeded the penalty.

Implementing the landscape plan loomed before us. We'd decided to drop courtyard landscaping from our contract with Green Hammer to escape their markup. There were experienced gardeners among us. We wanted to do at least some of the planting ourselves to save money and because we enjoyed it. Operating Manager Lavinia appointed a self-selected committee of Francie, John, Lainie and Carol to recommend a landscaping sub, manage its work and determine what we could do ourselves. Fruit trees in the courtyard? Other edibles? Plantings for bird habitat? Fruit or fall color from the street trees? How big should the vegetable garden be? [29]

One issue for the landscape committee was boat storage. Was there a place we could store them? Neither the condo storage nor each unit's patio storage could accommodate 19-foot kayaks and canoes. Every partner had at least one boat; some had three. The initial design called for storage in the carport above the cars. That idea succumbed to the city-required revisions to the carport design. Cages in the alley behind the back units was the next idea. But only three feet separated the building from the wall supporting the dentists' parking lot; not enough room to maneuver a long kayak. And storage there would require a gate in the fence to be built on the wall, to allow access to the boats, assuming the dentists would grant permission. The committee mulled and advised partners to store their boats off-site.

It was now July, 2014, peak season for construction, but activity seemed to slow. At times it seemed only Patrick was on the site, wandering around looking lonely. He said one of the carpenters had suffered a heart attack, and he'd had to subcontract for some framing and siding work. Stephen apprised us of new delays: copper stolen from the rear building had to

---

[29] See Chapter 5 for courtyard sketch.

be re-installed; heavy rain of late June collapsed one of the planter trenches; delivery of Forest Stewardship Council (FSC) timber was delayed due to high demand; slow production of trusses forced a shift to glue-lams, custom-built to meet seismic standards. He also explained the HardiePanel "exposed-edge" problem. Standard panels would not fit our buildings; each piece had to be cut, exposing an edge. Hardie would not warrant panels with exposed edges. GH proposed a metal edge over the cut. Some partners expressed concern over the appearance of a metal edge. Stephen said GH would paint the metal to subordinate them visually. He also said metal edges would increase panel endurance. Partners asked for a mock-up. The struggle to satisfy Hardie was just starting.

When it came time to install the solar panels, representatives of SynchroSolar (SS), installer gave us a tutorial on the PV system and state and federal tax credits and incentives. The panels were built in Malaysia by SunPower of Arizona, reputed to be the best manufacturer in the U.S. Panels are warranted for at least 80 percent productivity for 20 years, though panels usually last longer. By design, we could add panels later if needed.

SS said the panels could not operate until inverters - which convert DC current to AC - had been installed. Siding had to come first. Once installed and inspected, panel operation would begin. Each unit owner would establish a net metering agreement with Portland General Electric (PGE).

We understood that each home would receive individual state and federal tax credits, but the tax-credit picture for the six panels dedicated to the common room was cloudy. SS thought the LLC might be eligible for the credits. It would own the common room until "turnover" to the HOA. But the LLC generates no revenues and, hence, could not benefit from a tax credit. One idea was to reconfigure the metering so the output of the six panels would be distributed to the units, allowing each owner to claim 13 rather than 12 PVs. But we concluded the reconfiguration would cost more than the credit.

SS suggested filing for a "pass-through": the sale of the credit by the LLC to a unit owner or another entity. A third idea was to provide in the HOA Bylaws and Declaration that each unit owner also owned one-sixth of the panels metered to the common room. All agreed there

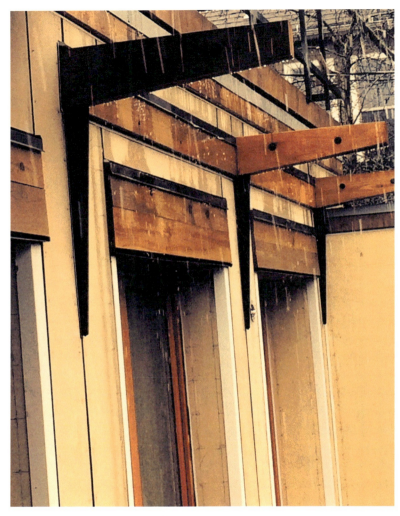
Boomerangs

was no point seeking legal advice because the cost of the advice would eat the modest credit. We gave up on credits for the common room panels.

The panels were installed as we debated anyway. Three days of work put the panel clips in place. By mid-July, all 78 panels were mounted on the south-facing slope of the Building B, clipped to the seams of the metal roof. They were so unobtrusive we had to look closely to notice them.

One fine day in July a neighbor living in the CoLab apartments to our west was overheard to say the "face" Ankeny Row presented to the CoLab courtyard was unattractive. The speaker was referring to the utility meters on the west end of the exterior wall of the storage unit. The neighbor was right; it was unlovely. Partner John Munson planted an espaliered pear along the west property line to screen it.

Building C rose steadily with the subcontracted carpentry crew at work. Framing was completed and trusses and sheathing began to appear. We'd heard Green Hammer use the term "boomerangs" and imagined something we could play with in the courtyard. Now they appeared on the façade of Building B, metal brackets that would support patio trellises. Rafter tails and roof brackets soon appeared on Building A. Early in August, forms for storage and trash enclosures were poured. Windows appeared in Building A. The flow-through planter in the courtyard was connected to the storm drain. Radon piping was installed in all buildings, required by the city despite the absence of radon on the site. The city inspected for sheer strength and passed all the buildings. Things seemed to be cooking.

Our development advisor Jessy toured a back unit and paid particular attention to the line at which the second-floor deck joined the building. "This is the junction over a first-floor living space most likely to leak." She advised us to ask for a mock-up of the layering of materials to seal it. Green Hammer invited Jessy to inspect it and she invited a moisture specialist to join her. He expressed concern with the "lay-up." Patrick made revisions on the spot. The expert also recommended a different material, ethylene propylene diene monomer (EPDM), but Green Hammer stuck with its initial choice, thermoplastic polyolefin fully-adhered underlayment (TPO). Partners were certain materials with such names would be completely impervious. Jessy again demonstrated the value of an owners' representative. Three rainy seasons later, no leaks.

Patrick provided a revised construction schedule with his weekly progress report. Despite the quick framing and sheathing of Building C and near perfect weather, the completion date slipped to the 3rd week of November. In an unusual outburst, he recounted his four hours spent with BDS bringing yet another inspector up to date on the project. "This guy is the ninth guy assigned to Ankeny Row." The city was still suffering from shrinkage of its planning and building staffs during the recession.

Bike parking took our attention at the end of August. City bike parking maven Sarah Figliozzi - known to partners as Lavinia's daughter - advised how best to accommodate the many cycle types in the bike storage room. Following her advice, we placed a six-bike horizontal floor rack along the north wall and three wall hangers each on the east and west walls. That provided each unit with two spots, as partners had agreed. Some partners had more than one bike per person. We saw the possibility of suspending another couple of bikes from the ceiling. Figliozzi thought that was possible. There would be competition for the extra spots. Who would get them? We punted this one for post-occupancy entertainment.[30]

It was now early September, and days grew shorter. The common room and apartment were now fully clad with protective coatings of Densdeck. The minisplits were roughed in at the back units. Partners met at Ankeny Row for the first time. Sitting in the common room on portable chairs, turned-up buckets and stacks of building materials, we went over construction progress and schedule, landscaping and legal documents. Asked if the current completion date – November 22 – would hold, Patrick looked at his feet and hedged. He thought Green Hammer would make it by the end of November.

Densglass Wrap

---

30 See photo of bike room in Chapter 3.

Hardie had thrown another wrench into the installation of the non-standard boards for the siding. Green Hammer developed a new mock-up, which cost time and money. Partners whispered to each other we were very happy to have a GMP contract.

The landscape committee reported it would hire Winterbloom (WB) from among three firms to do the planting design. The landscape committee recommended a drip irrigation system to serve the courtyard, with hose bibs to water plantings to climb the back fence, upper decks of each unit and trees on Ankeny Street. The irrigation timer would be hung on the wall in the bike storage room. We expanded the WB contract to install the irrigation system.

Stephen and Patrick suggested WB also pour the concrete for the walkways and paths in the courtyard so Green Hammer would not have to tunnel under them. Stephen agreed to transfer $10,000 from the SOV to the landscape work because it would have gone to courtyard concrete work in the SOV. Lavinia reminded partners the budget for landscaping was $35,000; it was clear we were going to do violence to the budget.

The landscape committee gave special attention to the patios of each unit. Patios are limited common elements, commonly owned but controlled by occupants. Partners settled on the size of each unit's patio, striving for "patio equity" and minimal encroachment into the common courtyard. All thought connectors from the front unit patios to the paths and walkways should be the same material as the patios, for aesthetics.

The committee recommended flexibility for patio plantings, but none should be out of scale or discordant with the courtyard. We debated pavers v. stamped concrete for the patios. Pavers would be more attractive, but likely more expensive. The committee promised comparative cost information.

Work went inside for sheet-rocking and finishes as weather got colder. There was little new to see outside. Michael ignited a vigorous email exchange by suggesting a water feature in the courtyard for wonderful sounds and happy birds. Lo! Might there not be more racoons and possums than birds? Wouldn't the noise disturb loungers on their patios? "OK with us if it's close to the Royce's unit." Michael, mildly shell-shocked, suggested postponing further discussion until after move in.

October's leaves were changing color and partners met with Green Hammer to discuss move-in and other matters. Stephen and Patrick spoke of difficulties coordinating subs to complete all the different tasks happening simultaneously on the site over the next two months. Stephen suggested we make certain we have accommodations for December. Patrick notched one point on the bright side: the city would allow occupancy unit by unit.

Given circumstances, partners assigned move-in priority to Roger and Anne. The date was approaching for their annual departure to Italy for Roger's three-month teaching gig. Next would be Units 4 and 3, as Lainie and Dave and Lavinia and Dick were facing termination of apartment leases. Facing no lease termination or imminent home sales, Francie and Michael and Carol and John offered to move in later. The episode was another indicator that co-housing was going to work for us.

We saw progress at the site: sheetrocking winding up; painting underway; tile and floors going in; cabinets and counters getting mounted. We observed the mock-up of the latest HardiePanel and HardiePlank installation technique, approved by manufacturer Hardie and the city. Hardie would warrant the installation. We agreed the panel installation looked fine, especially upon hearing that there was no choice. We were pleased to re-assert authority, on the placement of the screws to attach the panels: six-inch spacing on the panel edges and 24-inch spacing in the field of each panel, to minimize the visual impact. Over the next months, we would marvel at the slow and tedious installation of panels and planks, one piece at a time, delaying installation of the PV inverters. We wondered whether Green Hammer or the sub was responsible for the very considerable labor costs.

Exterior paint was more entertaining. Lavinia didn't have to appoint a committee; Anne and Carol named themselves and took command. We agreed to a darker color on the first story and a lighter color on the second. We also agreed to repeat the darker color at the clerestory level, creating a sandwich effect. But none of us was enchanted with the color offered. The taupe was a good match for the Maranti wood windows and doors and the dark-stained lintels, but the tone was too dark. The paint committee took note.

Paint Options

WB submitted a bid for all the plantings in the flow-through planters, the irrigation system, the lighting, the placement of the basalt stones and the paths and patios. It was a dazzling $75,000, eliciting groans from the assembled partners given the $45,000 in the budget. There was talk of value engineering for landscaping, but that had already happened. We could do some of the planting. Partners asked: "Could we do some of the irrigation placement?" As a practical matter, there was no juice left in the lemon.

Patrick dropped another bombshell: the city had hinted it would not issue occupancy permits until all the flow-through planters were planted. If not completed by November 1, planting could not re-commence until March, 2015. It was now October 9. Could WB do it all by the end of the month? Green Hammer said that effort might put things out of sequence and delay project completion. Lainie bravely said she and Patrick would "fix" the problem.

Lavinia alerted us to the seventh "call" for cash from partners, the last big one. A clause in the DBIA contract provided that once only 12.5 percent of total construction cost remained, Green Hammer would draw down the retainer submitted at the beginning. Once it was drawn down, there would be no payments on the remaining five percent until "substantial completion." Stephen said substantial completion did not include items on "punchlists", those small items that linger on after occupancy. Lavinia noted the squishy definition of "substantial completion" in the contract and warned of troubled water ahead.

In mid-December a dispute arose over HOA insurance. We expected our insurance to commence upon completion of construction. A Green Hammer email to their insurance broker about current coverage disturbed our expectation. Their Builders Risk insurance was due to expire December 27, following an expensive ($12,500) extension of 90 days from September 27. Their WRAP policy, including construction defect liability insurance, was set to commence coverage for the 10-year statutory period of repose that same date. Green Hammer was ready to represent to its broker that the project would be substantially complete, demonstrated by move-in on December 27 of three of the partners. The consequences would be that the LLC would have to start the HOA insurance on December 28. A further implication would be that the project was, in fact, "substantially complete" as defined in the construction contract, and no "liquidated damages" would accrue for failing to finish construction by the contract deadline ($250/day after December 18). Eventually, the partners waived any claim to such damages because move-in was within several weeks of the deadline.

The latest move-in forecast migrated to December 20, 2014. Anxiety waxed for the three partners facing expiring leases or teaching stints in Italy. Green Hammer promised to prioritize completion of their units. Patrick and Lainie persuaded the city to authorize occupancy before planting all the flow-through planters if at least one planter was planted.

Installation of the siding was about to begin. Green Hammer wanted to install with nails rather than screws to speed the process. No problem with warranty by Hardie, Stephen said. Partners, worried about the look, wanted another siding mock up.

Hardie Panel

Winterbloom (WB) suggested partners install nozzles on the irrigation system to save $2,200, more if we did some of the plantings. We decided to place the nozzles. But memories of staining the rafter tails brought us to our senses: let WB plant the plants. Lavinia informed us we were now at least $30,000 over budget for landscaping. But WB would do all the remaining work: plant the flow-through planters; pour the concrete walkways; install the boulders along walkways, plant the courtyard; set up the vegetable garden; plant trees on Ankeny Street; build the patios; install pavers to match patios on the courtyard terrace. We were tired, getting older and susceptible to the end-of-project syndrome. Leaving the balance of the work to WB seemed fine.

An intruder had come onto the site from the unfenced north side and deployed the fire extinguishers in the back units, despite there being no fire. We accelerated the process for installation of a fence atop the retaining wall for security along the north boundary.

November blew in and it was only a month before some of the partners were to move in. By all appearances their units would not be ready. Stephen sent an email:

> "I hear you loud and clear and completely understand the concerns….We all deserve more clarity about what can be expected regarding the schedule and budget. We especially need the clarity in regards to move in dates and coordination with Winter Bloom and the credits for the work they are taking over from Green Hammer…. We very much appreciate your business and are working hard to deliver the quality of work you deserve. In general Green Hammer has always emphasized fair wages and a strong work-life balance which is a challenge as we move into this crunch. We have authorized nearly one thousand overtime hours in the past few months to facilitate progress and we are keenly aware this has not been enough. There are many challenges to this project, which are very unique including project scope additions that are still coming in, which take away from our ability to manage for the finish line and have us focusing on individual unit service. This has been a tremendous learning experience for myself and my firm and we have evolved considerably because of this project. This cohousing community is a local and national treasure to show what can be done….We very much enjoy you all as clients and will be focusing on getting you the answers you need."

Partners appreciated Stephen's candor and applauded the Green Hammer workplace philosophy. Without thought about the consequences for the schedule, we'd asked Patrick to repaint a wall color that didn't satisfy, or change a showerhead stem from nine to six inches. We accepted a share of responsibility for completion creep.

Cabinets, tiles, counters and sinks in the back, sheetrock and paint in the front: there was lots of activity as GH pushed to meet its mid-December target. All eyes were on the fine details as finishes appeared. There were imperfections. There was a sloppy tile edge on the wall of Unit 3's master bath. Patrick and Josh, the tile installer, took time to make it right. A breakdown in communication between the designer and the builder brought Unit 4 a cabinet door that opened in a direction that construction would make impossible. Despite the stubbed toes from endless inspections, we were pleased with the quality of the work.

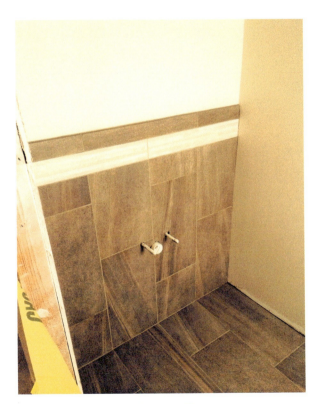

Bathroom Tile

Partners began to face a downside of the marvelous Zola windows: how to hang shades against the spring and fall sun when the windows tilt and swing inside? None was keen on the obvious answer: hang the shades on the outside of the building. Operating Manager Lavinia pursued the problem with specialists and Zola. Zola said it was OK to tack shades onto the inside wood strips sealing the panes. Another approach was to suspend shades from the walls above the windows and adjust them to swing or tilt the windows open. Most partners chose the first option.

Cabinet Installation

Partners came to the site on a chilly November day to select exterior paint and face Green Hammer again on the completion schedule. Paint came first. Paint mavens Anne and Carol persuaded us to reject the layer-cake look of different colors at the three building levels. With all the colors of wood and metal, layers would make facades too busy. They'd enlisted the services of a 'colorist.' She guided us to "Intellectual Gray" as the siding color. Unanimous approval! It seemed the paint's name reinforced partners' self-concept.

Stephen apologized for confusion over fixtures and appliances that had bedeviled the purchasing process. Frustrated with manufacturers, Green Hammer had attempted to buy things in the summer and store them. That would have avoided the discontinuation/re-selection problem or surfaced it earlier. The companies had discouraged this for warranty and insurance purposes. Stephen regretted heeding their advice, but discontinuation problems were now over. All fixtures and appliances had been purchased and were being delivered and stored.

GH took partners on a "walk-through" on December 4. We saw much progress toward occupancy. Electricity from PGE had been brought to each unit. Water service was expected by the end of the week. Appliances were being installed and the sidewalk on Ankeny was ready to be poured. Winterbloom had planted the interior flow-through planter on the west and passed city inspection. One hurdle remained in the path to occupancy: the bike bollard. We ordered it from Seattle.

Flow-through Planter

Patrick informed Lavinia of a BDS "incoming." The agency's water quality inspector was having second thoughts about her approval of the water retention system. She had approved but changed her mind. Her new look at the system revealed what appeared to her as a risk of backflow of domestic water into the pipe where it entered the property from the street. She said she wanted us to install a "backflow assembly" in the front planter. Patrick said WB was spending time at the Permit Center to find a solution. BDS's late change of heart would cost us money. But we were numbed to it. And occupancy seemed imminent.

CHAPTER 9: Moving In? "We can't stop you"

By Thanksgiving, 2014, it had become clear we would need to move in before the project was fully completed. The units were naked, as yet unclad by the coming HardiePanel and HardiePlank. Some of us were desperate. Leases were expiring; we were about to be tossed on the street and into the arms of generous friends with spare rooms. One set of partners faced imminent departure for a long-scheduled teaching gig overseas. The city had said we could move in unit-by-unit, allowing Green Hammer to prioritize their energies to the units of the desperados. But could partners move in before substantial completion? Could we move in if our unit had no siding?

The answer surprised everyone. Yes, we could move into a unit with no siding. The buildings were sealed— airtight and watertight— as a result of DensGlas gypboard and SIGA Membrane, the passive house wrap. But we could not move in until we'd met all the requirements of "occupancy": the city wouldn't issues certificates of occupancy until then.

Siga Membrane and Battens_

Follow-up question among partners: would we *want* to move into a construction site? Noise and mud came to mind. As of Thanksgiving the question was still premature. Green Hammer was moving as fast as it could. The sub installing the Hardie products was at work, albeit at snail's pace, nailing one piece of siding at a time. So, partners called for a meeting.

At the meeting, Alex Boetzel and Natalie Luttrell of Green Hammer were assigned to help Patrick coordinate remaining work and move-in dates. Alex said Units 3 and 4 would be ready no later than December 22. That was a problem for Lainie and Dave of Unit 4; they were leaving for Mexico on the 21st. Unit 1 would be ready January 16, which spelled trouble for Anne and Roger. They'd sold their condo and were leaving for his three-month teaching stint in Italy on January 12. If they couldn't drop their furniture in Unit 1, they would have to move their belongings into storage.

Bike Bollard

Green Hammer's highest priority, Stephen reminded us, was not accommodating our move-in hopes but the quality of work, which he would not compromise. None of us dared contest. Each of us looked away from the others. The oxygen drained from the room. Then Dave and Lainie offered to delay move-in until their return from Mexico. Oxygen was restored and brains began to function again. We would find solutions.

Later that day Patrick sent a revised schedule. It was good for Roger and Anne: they could move their worldly goods into Unit 1 just before their flight. Move-in for Unit 3 slipped from December 23 to December 28. That was OK, too: Dick and Lavinia were returning on the 28th from a family Christmas in D.C.

Winter became the enemy. Freezing weather forced Winterbloom (WB) to postpone paving courtyard walkways, a prerequisite to occupancy and moving furnishings to rear units. Crews swarmed over Units 3 and 4. But things slipped again. First occupancies now pushed into early January. Lainie and Dave felt panic all the way from Mexico. Movers were set to empty their condo and deliver its contents to Unit 4 on January 5. Alex said they could move their furniture into the unit upon their return. It would be close.

Several days into 2015 John picked up the bike bollard– another pre-requisite to occupancy– in Vancouver across the river. Next day, WB installed it at the corner of the common room. Only pouring the courtyard walkway stood between Units 3 and 4 and occupancy.

WB poured the main walkway in the courtyard on January 7. BDS inspected after 24 hours of concrete cure, and later that day, the city announced the following ringing 'thumbs up' to occupancy: "We can't stop you from moving into Units 3 and 4."

On Friday, January 9, 2015, Dick and Lavinia moved into Unit 3 and Lainie and Dave into Unit 4. We bobbed and wove among workers touching up paint, installing shelves in cabinets, placing the shields in front of the ethanol fireplaces and vacuuming the floors. The movers followed Patrick's plywood trails through the mud to the units. The new occupants flushed, cooked, slept, showered with hot water, heated the units and took evening walks through a well-concealed breach in the security fence.

At a regular billing meeting Stephen put us at ease on the meaning of that vague "substantial completion" term. It would come upon issuance by the city of certificates of occupancy for Units 6 and 7 (apartment and common room). Patrick scheduled a substantial completion meeting with each partner to compile the unit's "punch list." [31]

Green Hammer reminded partners of their commitment to "commissioning." Rather than simply handing keys to each partner and wishing us well, they would show us how to operate the HRVs, the mini-splits, our appliances, the water heater, everything with moveable parts or filters. Each partner would have a three-hour commissioning session. Recognizing we would forget frequencies of filter changes moments after 'learning' them, Green Hammer had prepared for each of us an owner's manual on a stick. Partners vowed to read the hundreds of pages of product manuals and be responsible owners.

Partners had questions about quotidian matters facing those living at a construction site. The site was still fenced and secured at night because there were lots of expensive tools in the

---

[31] Builders' term for the little things not yet done by the time of occupancy.

courtyard. What if Lainie wanted to walk the dog after hours? How could furniture movers get to the back units, through the widely scattered work centers and the sea of mud? "We'll work with you on this," Green Hammer promised…and did.

Living with Construction

And we learned about life at a construction site. Crews invaded at 7:30 and swarmed the site until 5:30 when Patrick turned out the lights. WB tamped gravel for the patios and common room terrace and put stones in place. The Hardie team cut panels and lap siding in the courtyard and hammered pieces into place. A third crew installed frames for the deck railings and welded metal sheets onto the frames. In the maelstrom we came to appreciate an unsung benefit of PH: our thick walls and triple-paned windows deafened us to the whining table saws and welding blasts. Anne and Roger dropped a truckload of furniture at Unit 1 on January 12 and caught their flight to Italy.

Construction Hardie Cutting

WB finished work on connecting walkways through the courtyard, trading places regularly with crews cutting fir strips, metal brackets and HardiePanel and HardiePlank for the siding. There was a new work-site configuration every day.

Francie and Michael moved into Unit 2 on February 2. There was a tussle over the kitchen sink. It was white. It was to have been brown. A drainage problem arose, threatening their cork floor. Green Hammer contended WB had unilaterally raised the grade in front of Unit 2 on the courtyard side, to slow drainage down the slope from Building B. To remediate, WB dug a French drain on the courtyard side of Unit 2.

The placement of hot water heaters in patio sheds caused problems. Green Hammer chose a particular high efficiency heater that would nestle nicely into the small shed. That model lost its efficiency certification on a technicality. They installed another, slightly larger heater. Soon thereafter, occupants heard dings and traced them to their sheds. Alex found that insufficient circulation around the heater triggered the filter alarm. The plumbing sub moved them for better circulation.

On February 10, Carol and John moved into Unit 5. We were a small village now, and began to visit one another across the courtyard. Neighbors started to share rides to the airport and gather in each other's units for meals. Recycling practices improved. Touted benefits of co-housing were realized.

Mid-February it finally got rainy, northwest Oregon style. Half-installed gutters sent water diving into deep mud pools in the courtyard, pocking WB's tidy landscape grading. Workers got soaked. Deck planking had appeared early February. Sheet-rocking of the patio storage units started the second week. The closer the project got to completion, the slower seemed the progress. Something to do with infinity. Yet, to hear occupants talk, life in the unfinished units was good.

Dust settled in the courtyard as the siding team moved to the Ankeny Street façade. Railings and decks showed up. Address numbers showed up on the common room facade. Patrick no longer had to flag down the UPS trucks and moving vans.

Lavinia told each partner it was time to open a net metering account with PGE in anticipation of "turning on" the PV panels. In late March, PGE announced the panels were feeding electricity generated onto the grid.

Customized pieces of siding were still going up in early March. The bike room opened for business and filled with bicycles. WB planted tupelos and magnolias in the strip along Ankeny Street. It was such a warm winter the trees showed their leaves a week after planting.

'Retired' furnishings from partners' former homes poured into the common room. Tableware, chairs, couches, chairs, art, card tables, a propane grill cluttered the room and terrace. Calls by the Common Room Committee (CRC) for certain items produced a substantial surplus. What if one partner thought another's table was ugly? Suppose one of us brought her beloved Aunt Agnes' "Still Life" for the wall above the side table and another of us thought it abhorrent? If we had three couches and needed one, which one? Would our dreams of co-housing comity break down over cast-offs?

One idea was to place the burden on the CRC, akin to sending military base closures to a commission whose decisions Congress could not touch. A worldly-wise partner advised us we should distance ourselves from the goods and simply speak our minds. "None of this is personal. We are adults; rather mature adults come to think of it. No one should be offended by rejection of her lamp." That worked, although a mild form of aggression surfaced among ordinarily mild-mannered people. An hour of slash and burn and it was all over. Partners sent rejected items to the kids, Goodwill, Albertina Kerr or the ReBuilding Center.

Settling in also meant exercising our new Bylaws. Of course, exercising them implied *reading* them. Former regulators among us – from city, regional or state governments – *did* read them and became oracles. A dog-owning partner wanted to build a low fence around their patio to keep Spot out of the courtyard proper. Another wanted to erect a peace pole in the courtyard, but Bylaws required approval. Partners said "maybe" to the fence, pending review of a design, and "no" to the pole because it would be in the courtyard, sacred ground. The pole was relocated to that home's patio, a "limited common element."

On April Fool's Day, partners installed irrigation hoses and nozzles in the courtyard while it rained. The job went on for a week. We saved a couple of thousand dollars and re-learned why even middle-aged people pay landscapers to do such things.

Partners Install Irrigation System

On the sun-splashed terrace of the common room, Stephen said Building C would be finished by the end of the week of April 13. He was ready to sell Unit 6, the apartment in Building C, at a price between $430,000 and 450,000. He was getting interest and promised us we would have an opportunity to 'vet' potential buyers.

WB's work on the landscaping was nearly complete. The total expenditures so far had been $94,000; the final cost, Lainie thought, would be $102,700, $14,000 more than the contract price and double the initial budget because of included additional work, such as the pear espalier on the west line, the fence on the east line, the runnel in the entryway, revisions to downspouts, installation of the bike bollard and extra gravel and bark dust.

Green Hammer organized a media tour of Ankeny Row for April 14. Two days after the tour articles started popping up: *Oregonian*; *The Business Journal*; *The Portland Tribune*; and several magazines. KGW and KATU sent reporters and cameras. Visitations to the courtyard by the curious jumped from the normal one or two parties a day to five or six. We welcomed them, most of whom were neighbors who'd endured 18 months of disruption. Also, there might be a buyer for Unit 6 among them. And we were preachers of the gospel of co-housing, net zero and aging in place. We cheerily answered questions. Nonetheless, the pace of informal visits rekindled the idea from the first site design for an un-gated entry portal (victim of "value engineering") to help people distinguish between the public and the private realms.

Warm, dry weather brought the first test of the courtyard irrigation system. Someone had failed to cap one of the spigots. The first turn-on resulted in a geyser and a quick turn-off. The irrigation genies found the exuberant spigot and stuffed it. The system then performed well.

Green Hammer produced the list of "change order" costs ("Additions Sheet") as a prerequisite for consideration of their retainer request, and we were generally comfortable with the itemization. There were a few other matters we wanted added– a punch list for the common room; commissioning; identification of outstanding customization costs; agreement on the start date of GH's one-year warranty– before the final payment under the contract, and before an LLC decision on liquidated damages for delay.

The cost of change orders and the steady billings for Winterbloom work on landscaping (and its increased scope) reminded us how the cost of our townhouses had again risen (see Chapter 7, Design-Build in Action). The cost of a "base" unit had escalated 15 percent from our initial estimate, excluding customization decided on by each homeowner for their own home. Five percent of this increase was due to underestimation for landscaping, lawyers, and permits. Ten percent of the increase was the rising costs of construction– materials and subcontractors – reflecting a housing market recovering from the Great Recession. By the end of construction, the base cost of the townhouses was $656,000.

The city issued certificates of occupancy for Units 6 (small condo) and 7 (common room) on April 28, 2015. This marked "substantial completion" of Ankeny Row, as determined by Green Hammer and accepted by the partners. Each of us signed a completion form; and but for punch list items, we were done.

Word had spread beyond partners that Unit 6 was for sale. Sue Best asked Stephen to show her around. Sue decided she wanted the unit and signed a month-to-month rental agreement. She made the round of partners, met universal acceptance and moved in mid-August, 2015. She expected to buy Unit 6 in a matter of months. It happened, but many more months than she or Stephen expected.

The duty punch list handyman for Green Hammer, Davey Beacom, arrived each morning at 7:15 and directed subs to the few remaining tasks, large and small. He fixed anything they couldn't or wouldn't.

Another consequence of moving in before everything was ready quickly became apparent. We were very pleased to be in; dwelling in our units made GH's high quality work and craftsmanship even more obvious, but we couldn't help noticing small imperfections. No sooner had Davey punched an item off our lists than we would add two more. For months after move-in, punch lists lengthened and shortened in perverse rhythm. For Green Hammer, "punch list" had taken on an ominous connotation.

The most vexing item was a surprise to everyone. Lainie and Dave, in the middle back unit, began to notice low level noises emitting from the west unit. With PH's thick walls we, and

Green Hammer, expected nearly complete silence from adjoining units. Testing revealed that the shared foundation was transmitting noise among the back units. They deployed a series of mitigation measures in the units, such as insulating electrical outlets in the common walls. They helped, but good behavior between neighbors proved the best muffler.

Alex 'commissioned' each unit with its occupants, who got a close look at all the filters they would have to clean. He presented each of us with our Owner's Manual; it answered every conceivable question about operation of the units. He also brought us Green Hammer's promise to remain available for support. They kept their promise so well some partners began to feel guilty (slightly).

CHAPTER 10: From Partners to Homeowners

Ankeny Row began life as a limited liability corporation (LLC). The LLC would have a limited life, too; we planned to dissolve it when Ankeny Row became a condominium. The lawyer-partners, with the wisdom gained from our partial DIY LLC experience, no longer suffered from the illusion that we could handle the condo documents all by ourselves, but nevertheless we plunged into the Oregon condo statute to learn how to do the conversion.

The statute called for a "turnover meeting" (from LLC to condo) within 90 days after four of Ankeny Row's six units had been sold. At the turnover, the LLC would present specified items to the owners and relinquish administrative control to an already-established homeowners association (HOA). At the meeting, the new HOA would elect a board of directors. The list of items was long, but seemed straightforward, ranging from site plans, blueprints and permits to financial statements and insurance policies. Two items, however, were critical (and required by the condo statute): the "reserve study" and the plat survey.

Partners Dine in Community Room

Operating Manager Lavinia hired CPA firm Schwindt & Company to do the reserve study, with the following objective: "The purpose of this study is to insure that adequate replacement funds are available when components reach the end of their useful lives."

The study would be the basis for owners' monthly dues to the HOA. Partners paid keen attention.

There are two components to the reserve study: an Operating Budget and a Maintenance Plan. The Operating Budget includes all annual expenses for common costs and ongoing maintenance, such as property and roof inspections, the fee for the fire suppression system, landscape maintenance, utilities (water and electricity) for common areas, garbage, cable service, maintenance of gutters and downspouts, insurance, tax prep for the Homeowners Association and bookkeeping.

The Maintenance Plan would address all systems and components – from the irrigation system to the roofs and siding - to determine life spans of each and estimated maintenance and replacement costs. A significant amount of monthly HOA dues would go to the reserve fund to carry out the Maintenance Plan.

Systems and materials had to be in place on the site before Schwindt could complete the study. This meant the study would start near the end of construction, which seemed to recede every time the subject came up.

Lavinia hired Chase, Jones to do the plat survey. It would show everything on the site and distinguish the individually-owned units from the "common elements," such as the courtyard and the bike storage, and "limited common elements," elements that are owned in common but are under partial control of individual owners, such as patios, decks and the photovoltaic panels. The county would use it to establish assessed values. Insurance companies would rely upon it to settle claims. And owners and the HOA would turn to it if there were a dispute over control of a space. This could start before the end of construction. Lavinia got it going in early spring of 2015. She soon regretted she hadn't started it much earlier.

Unbeknown to us, the survey required excruciating detail. Chase, Jones employees arrived at Unit 3 one day to survey the ceiling in the living room to show precisely where the exposed fir beams met the ceiling.

While awaiting the reserve study and the plat survey, we worked on documents for the yet-to-be-born Ankeny Row Condominium Owners Association (ARCOA), our HOA. The Articles of Incorporation, Declarations and Bylaws would have to be drafted by the lawyer-partners, repaired by our "real" condo lawyer, approved by partners and filed with Multnomah County and the State of Oregon. See Chapter 6, Documents, Documents. Iterations of each document bounced ping-pong fashion among the lawyers for weeks. Partners finally approved them in September, 2015, eight months after partners began to move into their units, but OM Lavinia could not file them until Chase, Jones completed the survey.

Chase, Jones warned us Multnomah County was "tough" on condo plat surveys; we should anticipate county corrections and more work by them. We didn't, however, anticipate the long game of "wrong rock" played between them and the county. After each rejection, they returned to Ankeny Row for additional measurements. Once it was the common room and attached storage. Then it was the patios, each of which was different. On another visit they re-measured the decks. Lavinia called Chase, Jones regularly to check progress. They said the three classes of ownership, and lots of "ins" and "outs," made Ankeny Row complicated. They started in January, 2015, but we did not receive county approval of the survey until October 2015. Then finally, we could file documents and emerge from the LLC chrysalis and turn into a beautiful condominium owners association.

The reserve study was a piece of cake in comparison. Schwindt mined records at Green Hammer to identify whether they or a subcontractor were responsible for each system and material. They determined the type and cost of materials used and the cost of the labor to build the item. For installed components, the study listed the manufacturer, the cost of the item, the installer and the cost of installation. Using a cash flow method and a threshold funding model, Schwindt estimated repair and replacement dates and costs for each item.

Schwindt sent us a draft in late Fall, 2015; it was encyclopedic. Metal roofs, bamboo, cork and maple floors, the Zola windows and doors, deck wood, the siding, the works. The metal roof, for example, costing $40,320 (materials and installation), had a lifespan of 40 years and would take $96,217 to replace in 2055. It was comforting to contemplate that it would likely be our successors-in-interest who would face replacements. A noteworthy element of the maintenance plan was the built-in 2.5 percent inflation rate.

Lavinia sent the draft study to partners, noting it would be the basis for determining monthly HOA dues. All eyes went to the number: $313, close to the number prior owners of condos among us had paid. Condo savvy partners suggested a way to reconcile ourselves to the dues: you should expect to pay a similar amount for short and long-term maintenance of a single-family dwelling. As such homeowners, none of the partners had set aside $313 a month for the future. Now we were required by law to do it, and we would be thankful later.

Deploying our green eyeshades we noted the absence from the study of property taxes. Other items, such as the cost of preparation of federal and state taxes, were too high or too low. Lavinia sent these and other suggested changes to Schwindt. We received the final study on December 1, 2015.

Our LLC/condo lawyer informed us she had filed the necessary HOA documents with the state and the county for recording.[32] The HOA was now a real legal creature. The LLC could now transfer title to unit owners. We'd each soon have that most coveted of documents: a deed. For Sue Best, our last partner, it meant she could finally buy Unit 6 from Stephen, who now had a deed to convey. She closed on March 2, 2016, seven months after renting, one week before the turnover meeting.

Naturally, the subject of insurance arose, and we reviewed bids for the different types of insurance for ARCOA, which differed from that required for the LLC. Partners approved the choice of insurer. Unit owners now became responsible for insuring the contents of their units. Lavinia recommended that owners buy insurance from the same company that insured ARCOA. In the event of spilled red wine on the window sill that flows inside and outside, only one company would be involved in the claim.

Our soon-to-be-retired Operating Manager Lavinia ensured that the deeds were prepared and assembled the critical papers of the HOA into the loose leaf folder that became Ankeny Row's Sacred Text. We rounded up the oversized materials from Green Hammer– construction drawings, for example– required by the condo statute. We were ready for turnover.

On March 9, 2016– two years and six months after Dr. Feist of the PassivHaus Institut helped partners break ground, one year after the last of the partners had moved in - Ankeny Row LLC turned control of the project over to Ankeny Row Condominium Owners Association. Partners gathered in the fully-furnished common room. Lavinia called the meeting of the LLC to order and handed deeds to new unit owners. She placed a small mountain of materials on the table and called upon partners for a motion to make the turnover official. It passed with Unit 6's

---

[32] Samples of a Declaration, Bylaws and Operating Agreement for ARCOA are available at https://ankenyrow. wordpress.com/

new owner Sue joining the cheer. Lavinia adjourned the LLC meeting, took a seat amid hearty applause and felt a heavy burden lifting from her shoulders.

Lainie, temporary chair, called the first meeting of the HOA to order. There was only one item on the agenda: election of the three-member board of directors. Lainie, Roger and Dick were elected unanimously by the other members, who were pleased they'd not been elected. Lainie adjourned the meeting and the party started.

CHAPTER 11: The First Two Years

The project had received press before and during construction, but attention to Ankeny Row boomed after we moved in.[33] On April 16, 2015, the Portland Business Journal published *Southeast Portland housing project approaches net-zero energy*, which reported "Green Hammer founder and CEO Stephen Aiguier and certified Passive House consultant Alex Boetzel led a tour of (Ankeny Row) this week."[34]

In the two years, many visitors inspected the new site. Twenty-six students in a sustainable building class from Osaka, Japan, visited, trooping through the project after taking off their shoes. Planners and city officials from Edmonton, Canada visited, groups from the American Association of Planners, American Architectural Association, and numerous other groups and individual tours swarmed the project for the first six months, tapering off to one or two a week after the first year.

The media and other attention occurred because the idea was ripe and attractive for a variety of reasons to many people. Beyond satisfying the owners' vanity, press coverage was warmly accepted because it meant that the ideas which had motivated Ankeny Row would become more widely known and perhaps replicated, which had been one of the hopes of the Ankeny Row partners from the start.

---

[33] For more pictures and background material on Ankeny Row see our blog. https://ankenyrow.wordpress.com/

[34] http://www.bizjournals.com/portland/blog/sbo/2015/04/energy-aces-unveil-power-friendly-southeast.html

Net Zero

In April 2015, Portland Tribune published an article entitled *Going net-zero in planned community*.[35] Dick was prominent standing in front of his house in the courtyard looking more like a lumberman than "a former senior attorney at Metro." The article focused on the passive house aspects. "Portland homebuilder Green Hammer used Passive House standards, which deploy superefficient insulation and other features to assure the units require minimal energy to heat and cool. Add in some solar panels for renewable energy, and the project doesn't produce any carbon emissions for its energy, earning it the net-zero label and assuring low utility bills."

An article in Oregon Home Magazine also stressed features leading to net zero. "Ankeny Row is designed to achieve net-zero energy status, giving its owners, all at or nearing retirement age, a chance to age in place without piling up utility bills. 'Our electric bill was $11 last month, and really, that charge was just for being connected to the grid,' says Lainie Smith, who lives at Ankeny Row with her husband, David Siegel." With the added insulation and triple-pane windows, the home is comfortable year-round without relying on much heating and cooling. "Our house just seems to want to be 72 degrees year-round," she added."[36]

In *Passive House Northwest 2016*, Ankeny Row was one of the 45 Passive House (PH) projects in Idaho, Oregon, and Washington featured. The article focused on PH construction features:

> "By using the Passive House Planning Package to sharply reduce each building's demand, the cohousing community is on track to achieve its goal of being Net Zero Energy, with only a 25-kW photovoltaic system on the back building's south-facing roof.

---

[35] http://portlandtribune.com/sl/257501-126100-going-net-zero-energy-in-planned-community
[36] http://www.oregonhomemagazine.com/homes/item/1017-apartment-and-condos-learning-to-fit-in

The community's three buildings were sited so the courtyard could get the most sun penetration, and great consideration was also given to maximizing the building's solar heat gains in winter while preventing overheating in summer. Deep overhangs shade the large, south-facing windows on the topmost floor, while awnings protect the lower and ground-floor windows. For supplemental heating and the small amount of cooling needed, all units come equipped with mini-split heat pumps."

Reviewing our electricity consumption since we moved in, the partners were gratified to see that our development still achieved net zero, generating more than was consumed in the first two years, even with common room consumption and generation.

Ankeny Row: Electricity Usage

	unit #1		unit #2		unit #3		unit #4		unit #5		unit #6	
	generated	consumed	generated	consumed	generated	consumed	generated	consumed	generated	consumed	generated	consumed
2015												
3/16-4/14	269	78	380	158	253	120	226	174	225	165	incomplete 2015 data	
4/14-5/14	430	162	376	135	447	119	457	201	448	177		
5/14-6/15	479	161	571	87	522	88	438	192	440	230		
6/15-7/15	559	159	494	205	580	79	535	153	537	205		
7/15-8/13	506	177	512	180	533	79	492	153	491	160		
8/13-9/15	450	207	352	224	441	140	432	184	409	272		
9/15-10/14	321	258	245	217	326	128	311	199	309	235		
10/14-11/12	139	304	89	272	150	154	135	251	142	226		
11/12-12/15	87	504	71	430	82	269	80	425	89	333		
12/15-1/15	63	593	59	499	69	274	58	487	47	511		
1/15-2/15	106	242	86	322	91	248	84	345	71	432		
2/15-3/15	173	180	170	261	154	205	142	285	133	297		
Totals	3582	3025	3405	2990	3648	1903	3390	3049	3341	3243		
Net surplus	557		415		1745		341		98			
2016												
3/14-4/15	364	133	359	175	347	150	325	203	306	220	349	220
4/13 - 5/12	409	245	373	141	436	139	408	177	405	158	441	158
5/12 - 6/13	447	227	439	189	473	99	422	168	406	186	453	186
6/14 - 7/13	454	189	427	194	460	109	419	183	452	152	461	152
7/13 - 8/11	458	151	450	223	486	73	435	150	430	174	469	174
8/11 to 9/12	492	101	403	234	516	90	459	166	465	180	487	180
9/12 to 10/11	254	161	243	116	297	91	254	205	252	202	298	202
10/11 to 11/9	133	204	96	237	130	177	127	210	127	248	147	248
11/9 to 12/12	63	371	60	468	80	340	62	392	51	494	98	494
12/12 to 1/12	59	544	37	599	70	453	76	425	61	510	78	510
1/12 to 2/10	67	243	97	383	53	412	41	542	38	544	56	544
2/10 to 3/14	174	224	126	362	160	274	151	307	130	394	172	394
Totals	3374	2793	3110	3321	3508	2407	3179	3128	3123	3462	3509	3462
Net Surplus	581		-211		1101		51		-339		47	
2017												
3/14 to 4/12	240	134	225	204	219	184	204	243	200	287	243	266
4/12 to 5/11	327	178	375	89	348	155	338	183	319	234	359	240
5/11 to 6/12	437	166	426	240	479	125	444	185	453	172	492	230
6/12 to 7/12	507	135	594	137	525	107	474	149	487	142	521	208

Co-housing

The Tribune article had highlighted that "Ankeny Row also is a co-housing community, whose residents share a garden, courtyard and common room." Two months after the last of the partners had moved into the project and while the project still looked somewhat naked and new, Elliot Njus authored an article for the Oregonian, *Wary of retirement housing options, some baby boomers make their own way*, which developed that theme: "We had lived in these big houses and we wanted to downsize in an environmentally sustainable way," said Francie Royce, who with her husband Michael, had initiated the Ankeny Row project with Benner and Gordon. "And we wanted to live with friends."[37]

Later in the September 2015 issue of Portland Monthly, a story featured the project: *How a Bunch of Retirees Created Portland's Greenest Communal Housing Outpost.*[38] The partners were arranged in the common courtyard in what strained to appear as an informal sunny afternoon gathering, but, of course, had been carefully staged by the photographer. Understatement is not the mode of this type of magazine piece which concluded: "Turns out, a bunch of retired city planners and lawyers have dreamed up one of the city's most ambitious, unorthodox living arrangements: a cohousing community that sits at the nexus of the city's density issues, the aging-in-place movement, and sustainable design."

Aging in Place

Our aging in place has continued and we have had two hip replacements and one new shoulder with another coming up. As is no surprise with a demographic now between 64 and 72, one partner experienced heart problems, and several have had brushes with cancer. When

---

[37] http://www.oregonlive.com/business/index.ssf/2015/04/wave_of_retiring_baby_boomers.html

[38] http://www.pdxmonthly.com/articles/2015/10/5/portlands-greenest-communal-housing

we moved into Ankeny Row, three partners worked full time and two others part-time. Now only one still works full time and the others wind down.

Everyone still bikes on a regular basis to the many social and volunteer activities in which we are involved, such as a wage claim group for low income workers, an international development non-profit, the board of a Farmer's Market, a trails advocacy group and a policy group raising consciousness about global warming. Yoga remains a Friday morning fixture even if we move more slowly. During the summer, many evenings find neighbors sharing impromptu meals or visits with a bottle of wine in the evening. In the common room, we share viewings of celebrated movies such as Cinema Paradiso and have the ten-part series of Ken Burns and Lynn Novick on the Vietnam War on our agenda. The small courtyard garden, supplemented by second story porch planters, provides more vegetables than we can consume.

Conclusion

"We'd been talking about 'shrinking our footprint;' and by that we meant more than downsizing," said Roger Chope as he considered the changes in his life. "It is really about taking less space on this earth." Anne, his wife added, "I come and go through the courtyard, not my front door on Ankeny, to see what's happening."

Another partner said, "People ask me what it's like to live so close to people. In previous neighborhoods, I really did not do much with neighbors. Here there is more contact and design plays a big part of that. You want to be close enough to feel like interacting and not so close that you feel you are looking into each other's living room. We've got that balance here."

"A variety of spaces is important. I'll have a drink with Dave out on the patio and wave at neighbors, but if I want more privacy, I go to my second floor porch," Lainie Smith said. "Social stuff isn't programmed." Her husband summarized our group experience best: "I feel closer to everyone here than I thought I would. It feels like a family."

Carol Munson commented on the balance between privacy and community. "I'm one of the introverts, whereas John is a big time extrovert. I am not big on dropping in. I can be in my own home with my own quiet time or go to the common room and watch Downton Abbey with neighbors." And thinking about the future, she added: "We do many activities with members of Ankeny Row, but all of us have active lives and travel a lot. As we get older, our situations and abilities will change and we will spend more time at home. That'll mean changes to the balance between community and privacy."

Life is change and our way of living at Ankeny Row will also alter. But for the moment, we are happy and look forward to how our community will evolve over time.

Chapter 12: Could You Do it for Less?

Is it possible to build something like Ankeny Row at lower cost? It's a question we ponder because we hope others will try.

Ankeny Row (AR) cost more than we anticipated. No one is surprised when we tell them: almost all construction projects cost more than initial estimates. But the initial partners knew before we got the first estimates that the units would be expensive. We had set goals for the project that would make it more expensive than ordinary construction. Green Hammer told us at the outset that building to passive house standards costs 10 to 15 percent more than building to city code standards. We were prepared to pay to achieve our goals. We were fortunate to find other partners who shared our values and had the resources needed to build to our goals.

Now that the dust has settled, we believe the answer is "Yes, you can do it for less." Even without abandoning the goals we set or sacrificing amenities. We'll be bold: today in Portland you could build something akin to Ankeny Row for almost $100,000 less than we paid (and a greater reduction if in parts of the country where land and construction are cheaper).

How Much Did Ankeny Row Really Cost?

Before we set forth the ways you could build for less, there is an important point to make about cost. When people ask what we paid for one of the townhouses, we give them the short answer and watch their eyebrows rise. The short answer: the five townhouses ranged from $650,000 to $690,000 (the smaller unit is significantly less).

Then we offer a fuller answer. Each unit is designed to passive house standards with all the advantages, including reaching net zero (no electricity bill except an $11 a monthly administrative fee). If passive house construction added 10 percent to our total construction costs of $2,880,440, then each townhouse would cost $590,000 to 630,000 while built to the same design, with all the amenities of our current project except passive house construction.

In addition, the development bears the cost of amenities usually not available to townhouses in traditional settings. We have a common room that is in constant use and large for six homes. It's a yoga studio for owners once or twice a week; a classroom for Spanish; the venue for many fundraisers and meetings of nonprofit boards. We watch movies, hold potlucks, host business meeting for those of us still working, big meals for member's families, reading the Sunday *Times* with coffee in hand. And just outside is the common room terrace, used regularly for barbecues and other gatherings.

We have a secure bike storage room for our fleet. We have storage cages like those found at high-rise condos. There is a shed for garbage, compost and recycling and garden tools. We have a generous courtyard that is the center of our social life, with a fecund vegetable garden. We have very private second-floor decks that look over the courtyard. And each townhouse has a first floor patio paying onto the courtyard, screened from other patios by courtyard vegetation.

Appraisers have difficulty assigning a dollar value to specific items within the overall construction, but we've come to value them more highly than we imagined during design. Take away some of these things and the cost of a townhouse would drop approximately $70,000.[39]

Lowering Price/Maintaining Vision and Goal

But we promised you could replicate AR for apporimately $100,000 less *without* sacrificing goals or amenities similar to ours. During the schematic design and design development stages,

---

[39] Estimated Values of some of the amenities, split among the six units: common room, $45,000; bike room $8,500; storage room, $8,500; recycling barn, $5,000; decks, $3,000.

partners and Green Hammer devoted many hours on "value engineering," trying to bring the cost down. See Chapter 5, Paying for Paradise. Those efforts are the source of many of the ideas here while other possible areas of reduction have sprouted from several years of living at AR and from the emergence of new products at lower cost. So here are our ideas:

Site

- We could have chosen a site that met our fundamental neighborhood criterion– walkability– farther from the center of Portland where there are also highly walkable neighborhoods with grocery stores and other retail three or four miles from the center and saved $100,000 on property, notwithstanding the great deal we got on our close-in site thanks to the Great Recession.
- We learned after we acquired the site– from the developer of the adjoining site– that soils on our site were unconsolidated because of a streambed filled early in the 20th century before the city required compaction, requiring 158 pilings to support the three buildings. See Chapter 8: Tonka Toys Arrive. Without that problem, we would have avoided the $80,000 cost of pilings or we could have negotiated for a reduction in the land sale price at our current location.

Design

- If we had made important decisions earlier such as not providing parking, a spa or hot tub – all inconsistent with our values– Green Hammer design time would have been reduced. Before we started construction, as we brought new partners in to share the cost of "design development" and to encourage a sense of "ownership," we allowed latitude in customization whereas in a more traditional model, customization would have been severely limited. More standardization would have delighted Green Hammer and made the whole process easier and cheaper. These changes could have reduced design costs from 12.5 percent of overall construction budget to a range of 9-10 percent, more typical of projects our size, saving $26,600 or 20 percent of design costs.

- Once the city learned that soils on our site were unconsolidated, BDS informed us we would not be able to "retain" rain water on our site. Instead, we would have to "detain" it: slow it's drainage into the storm water system. This was a double whammy: build flow-through planters *and* pay for storm drainage. By the end of the second year, we learned that, despite our soils, water stays on site and does not discharge into the storm water system. With more experience with storm water retention and detention, the city might no longer require flow-through planters, a saving of $43,000.

Customization: Materials, Furnishings and Fixtures

- Green Hammer offered us "base" appliances, fixtures and furnishings of a high quality in a set floor plan. But every unit had some "customization" of the floor "base floor" plan, such as replacing a guest bathroom with a wine cellar, and furnishings such as walnut lintel above the fireplace as opposed to fir. Such customizations averaged $29,000 per unit or $174,000 in savings.

- Most partners selected at least some of their own appliances and fixtures at even a higher grade and paid the difference. If we had coordinated our selections of appliances, lighting and plumbing fixtures, counter tops and other finishes, GH could have negotiated more favorable wholesale prices for bulk purchases. Potential savings: $18,000.

- Although Green Hammer offered a wide range of cabinets and shelves, shop-built and paint-grade by Parr Lumber, and all high quality, partners opted for hand-crafted and paint-grade Douglas fir built by Urban Timberworks and added decorative ceiling beams. Savings: $12,000.

- Out of concern units would not have enough storage, most partners raised kitchen cabinet and room storage to the ceiling instead of standard height with plain rather than Shaker doors. Potential savings $18,000.
- Ethanol fireplaces, a purely decorative feature cost $6,000 per unit.

Cost Saving Recommendations from Green Hammer

- If we had accepted more recommendations Green Hammer made during value engineering, we would have saved considerably.
    - Asphalt shingles rather than standing-seam metal on the roofs would have saved $35,000.
    - Finishing the common room ceiling with fir boards rather than sheetrock cost $2,000.
    - Pouring concrete for patios and the common room terrace rather than installing individual pavers would have saved $6,000.
    - Coordinating lighting and plumbing fixtures, counter tops and other finishes to save $2,000.
- We installed the best windows, doors and heat recovery ventilators (HRVs) available, imported from Europe. U.S. companies now match the standards of the products we installed and they cost less. Potential savings $11,000 per unit.
- If younger, we would have contributed more sweat equity to keep costs down such as the $1,000 saved by staining a small portion of the cedar rafters. Ambitious DIYers could save more by staining all the exposed cedar, taking on interior wall painting, and an increased portion of the landscaping. Savings $15,000.

The total project savings from the above items would be $553,200, or about $100,000 less for the five two-story units, and slightly more than half that for the smallest unit. This would have resulted in the five townhouses costing $550,000 to $590,000 within the range of the initial estimate.

We chose, however, to upgrade significantly from the base price because each of us had sold larger homes. The above estimates show how homes with the essential quality and amenities of our project could be built for significantly less.

Appendices

Appendix 1

Biographies of Ankeny Row Partners

Dick Benner

After law school, Dick became a staff attorney at 1000 Friends of Oregon, an advocacy organization founded to support and defend Oregon's new land use law requiring cities to establish growth boundaries beyond which land is protected for agriculture and forestry. He spent four years as director of the Columbia River Gorge Commission, guiding the adoption of the first management plan for the new Columbia River Gorge National Scenic Area. Later, he was the director of the Land Conservation and Development Department managing the state's land use program for ten years, shaping his thinking about what makes communities sustainable.

Michael Royce

Michael co-founded Royce, Swanson, Thomas, & Coon, a law firm and represented workers in suits to obtain compensation for injuries resulting from toxic exposure from 1979-1995. In

1986, he joined the board of a small family business with a working interest in two small run-of-the-river hydroelectric facilities. He and his wife founded Green Empowerment[40] to support isolated rural villages in Asia and Latin America in establishing renewable energy and potable water systems, serving over 20 years alternatively as Program Manager, Executive Director and Board Chair.

Francie Royce

Francie worked 23 year as a transportation planner and project manager with the City of Portland. Since retirement, she co-founded npGreenway[41], an advocacy group working to extend the Portland East Bank Esplanade ten miles north along the Willamette River to the confluence with the Columbia River and has served as a board member of Green Empowerment for the past 16 years. She and Michael live part time in the Columbia Gorge where she represents Wasco County on the Historic Columbia Highway Advisory Committee.

Lavinia Gordon

While practicing law and raising a family in the eighties, she served on the board of the Oregon Environmental Council. Later, she promoted biking, walking and transit for the Portland Bureau of Transportation where she met Francie. While managing the Transportation Options Division, and then the Bureau of Transportation Systems Management, Lavinia helped implement Sunday Parkways and the SmartTrips programs to help Portlanders make smart transportation choices. She currently serves on the board of Climate Solutions, a nonprofit dedicated to reducing global warming.

---

[40] www.greenempowerment.org
[41] http://npgreenway.org/

David Siegel

David Siegel followed his passion for facilitating change through a forty-year career in city and regional planning. Committed to working with governments, organizations and citizens to envision and develop strategies for achieving a desired future, Dave has worked locally, nationally and internationally on long term plans for vibrant downtowns, neighborhoods, communities and regions, and the strategies for carrying them out over time. Dave saw Ankeny Row as an opportunity to "walk the talk" about sustainability, "density done right", and being able to age in place in a neighborhood where everyone had each others' back.

Lainie Smith

Lainie Smith attended graduate school at Oregon State University where she earned a degree in geography. She followed her passion for the environment through a 30+ year career working for local and state government, eventually focusing on connecting transportation and land use. She dreamed of putting together a community of friends who would share their lives together and feels blessed that she found that community at Ankeny Row. She loves dogs, hiking, gardening, kayaking, travel, yoga, good food and wine with friends.

Carol and John Munson

Carol and John were committed early to the vision "small is beautiful" after reading E.F. Schumacher's book (1973). They both attended Dickinson School of Law, after which they practiced for a number of years. When their children (three biological, four adopted, and numerous foster children) were grown, they made new career choices: John as a high school teacher; Carol as a counselor at a residential treatment center. After retirement, they both joined the Peace Corps and served in Botswana. On returning from Africa, they looked for a unique urban "place of their own" before they learned about Ankeny Row. And now, after living here for more than two years, they feel they are part of the future.

Anne Morrow

Anne, a Portland native, left Portland to study political science at college. Ankeny Row has anchored her back in the town where she grew up. In the years between, she worked in several cities in many capacities but especially loved work as a Director of a Downtown Development with ties to the National Trust for Historic Preservation, consulting with cities and serving a first chair of Livable Oregon. Her final working years were with publicly owned utilities such as the Emerald People's Utility District and the Bonneville Power Administration. She still watches home movies from the 50's of her riding her bike on the Alameda Ridge and is so happy to be here.

Roger Chope

Roger taught accounting and statistics mostly in Oregon and Italy, where he still teaches every year. He also served on a number of not-for-profit boards, including those serving people with developmental disabilities and those involved with sustainable agriculture. In the process, he developed a fondness for cooking and for being outdoors, whether in a canoe, running, or on a bicycle. As it came time to shrink his footprint, both physical and carbon, the opportunity at Ankeny Row materialized, providing a chance to live near downtown and be part of a community of people who were committed to living responsibly.

Sue Best

Sue is a Chicago native (and Cubs fan!) who fell in love with the Northwest in her 20's and has called Portland her home ever since. Sue continues to follow her calling by working in health care is a palliative care social worker. Additionally, Sue serves as a deacon in the Lutheran Church. She is passionate about cycling and dragon boating. Sue is a member of the Pink Phoenix Dragon Boat Team, the first team in the US composed of breast cancer survivors. Sue is also engaged in other civic activities with a focus on social justice. Being part of the Ankeny Row community has been a true gift for Sue. She is excited to see what the future holds.

Appendix 2

ANKENY ROW TIMELINE

January, 2008:	Initial partner couples Francie and Michael Royce and Lavinia Gordon and Dick Benner (FMLD) acquire Tillamook Street property
March, 2008:	FMLD establish Tillamook LLC
Spring, 2009:	SOLARC Design/Engineering presents design concept
Summer, 2009:	Great Recession sinks project and partnership FMDL sell interest in Tillamook property
December, 2010:	FMLD acquire property on Ankeny Street
January, 2011:	FMLD demolish abandoned industrial building on the site
Spring, 2011:	FMLD interview design and design-build firms
Spring, 2011:	Design charrettes with three firms
May, 2011:	FMLD select Green Hammer (GH)
August, 2011:	FMLD and GH begin "schematic design"

October, 2011:	"Value Engineering" to reduce project costs
February, 2012:	Banks say no construction loan
March, 2012:	Ankeny Row LLC is born
April, 2012:	FMLD release Ankeny Row marketing package Francie and Michael choose Unit 2, Lavinia and Dick Unit 3
April, 2012:	Lainie Smith and Dave Siegal make deposit on Unit 4
May, 2012:	Roger Chope and Anne Morrow make deposit on Unit 1
December, 2012:	Carol and John Munson make deposit on Unit 5
December, 2012:	GH owners Stephen Aiguier and Karen Steer make deposit on Unit 6
February, 2013:	FMLD transfer their interests in property to Ankeny Row LLC
February, 2013:	New partners make capital contributions and join LLC
February, 2013:	Partners and GH begin "design development"
April, 2013:	Operating Manager Lavinia Gordon hires Jessy Olson as partners' representative
August, 2013:	Partners and GH begin second round of value engineering
September, 2013:	Dr. Wolfgang Feist of Passivhaus Institute breaks ground at Ankeny Row with partners
October, 2013:	City of Portland issues building permits for Ankeny Row
October, 2013:	Construction begins
December, 2013:	Partners and GH sign construction contract with guaranteed maximum price

January, 2014:	Framing rises on Building B
July, 2014:	Photovoltaic panels installed
September, 2014:	Partners adopt HOA articles, declarations and bylaws
December, 2014:	Schwindt & Co begins Reserve Study
January, 2015:	HOA is established by recording with Multnomah County
January, 2015:	Lavinia and Dick move into Unit 3 Dave and Lainie move into Unit 4
January, 2015:	Chase, Jones begins plat survey
February, 2015:	Francie and Michael move into Unit 2 John and Carol Munson move into Unit 5
March, 2015:	Solar electric system goes online at Portland General Electric
April, 2015:	Anne Morrow and Roger Chope move into Unit 1
April, 2015:	Media tour of Ankeny Row
April, 2015:	City of Portland issues final occupancy permits Ankeny Row is "substantially complete"
August, 2015:	Aiguier sells Unit 6 to Sue Best who rents until deeds issued by LLC
March, 2016:	LLC turns control of Ankeny Row over to Ankeny Row Condominium Owners Association (ARCOA) and issues deeds Partners in LLC become owners of condos

Printed in the United States
By Bookmasters